P9-DZM-638

Volume **10** **THE GOLDEN BOOK ENCYCLOPEDIA**

Jackson to lynx

An exciting, up-to-date encyclopedia in 20 fact-filled, entertaining volumes

Especially designed as a first encyclopedia for today's grade-school children

More than 2,500 full-color photographs and illustrations

From the Publishers of Golden® Books

Western Publishing Company, Inc.
Racine, Wisconsin 53404

©MCMLXXXVIII
Western Publishing Company, Inc.

All rights reserved

GOLDEN®, GOLDEN BOOK®, GOLDEN & DESIGN® and THE GOLDEN BOOK ENCYCLOPEDIA®
are trademarks of Western Publishing Company, Inc. No part of this book may be reproduced
or copied in any form without written permission from the publisher.
Printed in the United States of America.

ILLUSTRATION CREDITS
(t=top, b=bottom, c=center, l=left, r=right)

1 r, Sandy Rabinowitz/Publishers' Graphics; 3 bl, New York Public Library Picture Collection; 4 tl, Brown Brothers; 4 br, Culver Pictures; 6, Mike Yamashita/Woodfin Camp; 7 tl, Fred Mayer/Woodfin Camp; 7 br, Culver Pictures; 8, Chuck Fishman/Woodfin Camp; 9, Gary Lippincott/Publishers' Graphics; 10 bl, Robert C. Hermes/National Audubon Society Collection/Photo Researchers; 10 inset, John Lidington/Photo Researchers; 11, Louis Goldman/Photo Researchers; 12, Bettmann Archive; 13, Scala/Art Resource; 14 t, Brad Hamann; 14 cl, Arthur Sirdofsky; 14 inset, Richard Hutchings; 15, David Lindroth Inc.; 16 t, Sandy Rabinowitz/Publishers' Graphics; 16 inset, Richard Hutchings; 17, Fred Ward/Black Star; 18–19 b, Robert Frank/Melissa Turk & The Artist Network; 19 tr, T.E. Thompson/SPL/Photo Researchers; 20 br, David Lindroth Inc.; 22, Brown Brothers; 23 t, Jeffrey D. Smith/Woodfin Camp; 23 inset, Lloyd P. Birmingham; 24 tl, Van Bucher/Photo Researchers; 24 tr, H. Armstrong Roberts; 25, Gregory G. Dimijian, M.D./Photo Researchers; 26 t, NASA; 26 inset, David Lindroth Inc.; 27 bl, Juan Barberis/Melissa Turk & The Artist Network; 29 tr, Marilyn Bass; 29 bl, Cotton Coulson/Woodfin Camp; 30 tl, Bettmann Archive; 31, Elliott Erwitt/Magnum; 32 tr, Marilyn Bass; 33 bl, Frank J. Miller/Photo Researchers; 34 bl, David Lindroth Inc.; 34 br, Susan McCartney/Photo Researchers; 35 cl, Harriet Phillips/Lillian Flowers, Artists' Representative; 35 br, Focus on Sports; 36, © 1966 Flip Schulke; 37 bl, Scala/Art Resource; 37 br, Pierre Vauthey/Sygma; 39 br, Ken Ross/Viesti Associates; 41 tl, Kim Newton/Woodfin Camp; 41 bl, Martti Kainulainen/Woodfin Camp; 42, UPI/Bettmann Newsphotos; 43 br, Dave Healey/Sygma; 44–45 b, Dennis O'Brien/Joseph, Mindlin & Mulvey; 45 tl, Dan Guravich/Photo Researchers; 46, Tom Zimberoff/Sygma; 47 tl, Frank Mayo; 48, Frank Mayo; 49 tl, Graphic Chart & Map Co.; 50 tr, © Hank Morgan/VHSID Lab/ECE Dept., University of Massachusetts/Science Source/Photo Researchers; 50 bl, Southern Illinois University/Photo Researchers; 50 br, Chuck O'Rear/Woodfin Camp; 52 tr, Brown Brothers; 52–53 b, E.R. Degginger/Bruce Coleman Inc.; 53 tr, Michael O'Reilly/Joseph, Mindlin & Mulvey; 54, Biophoto Associates/Science Source/Photo Researchers; 56, Sandy Rabinowitz/Publishers' Graphics; 57, Michael O'Reilly/Joseph, Mindlin & Mulvey; 58 bl, Leo de Wys Inc.; 58 br, David Lindroth Inc.; 59 tl, The Museum of the Confederacy, Richmond, Virginia; 60 tr, Culver Pictures; 60 br, David Lindroth Inc.; 62, David Lindroth Inc.; 63, Philadelphia Convention & Visitors' Bureau; 64 t, Richard Hutchings; 64 inset, Lloyd P. Birmingham; 65 br, David Lindroth Inc.; 66 tl, Pierre Boulat/Woodfin Camp; 68, Fiona Reid/Melissa Turk & The Artist Network; 69 bl, Mei-Ku Huang, M.D./Evelyne Johnson Associates; 69 br, Michael O'Reilly/Joseph, Mindlin & Mulvey; 70 bl, Neal & Molly Jansen/Shostal Associates; 70 br, George Goodwin/Shostal Associates; 70 insets, David Lindroth Inc.; 71 tl, D.R. Bridge/Woodfin Camp; 71 br, Gary Withey/Bruce Coleman Inc.; 72–73 (art), Tom Powers/Joseph, Mindlin & Mulvey; 73 (photo), Focus on Sports; 74 tl, David Lindroth Inc.; 74 br, Gary Withey/Bruce Coleman Inc.; 75, Gary Lippincott/Publishers' Graphics; 76 tr, Brown Brothers; 76 b, Bettmann Archive; 77 tr, Brown Brothers; 77 bl, Bettmann Archive; 78, Juan Barberis/Melissa Turk & The Artist Network; 79, Frank Mayo; 80 both, Bettmann Archive; 81 both, The Episcopal Radio-TV Foundation; 82, Martha Swope; 83, Washington Square Press; 84, Harriet Phillips/Lillian Flowers, Artists' Representative; 85, Lloyd P. Birmingham; 86–87 t, Fiona Reid/Melissa Turk & The Artist Network; 86 bl, W.H. Amos/Bruce Coleman Inc.; 87 br, Francois Gohier/Photo Researchers; 88–89 t, Ken Ross/Viesti Associates; 88 bl, E.R. Degginger/Bruce Coleman Inc.; 89 br, Brown Brothers; 90 tr, Craig Aurness/Woodfin Camp; 91 both, Art Resource; 92 tr, G. Holton/Photo Researchers; 93 cr, Marilyn Bass; 94, David Lindroth Inc.; 95, Harriet Phillips/Lillian Flowers, Artists' Representative; 96 tl, Bettmann Archive; 96 br, Juan Barberis/Melissa Turk & The Artist Network.

COVER CREDITS

Center: Biophoto Associates/Science Source/Photo Researchers. Clockwise from top: Tom Powers/Joseph, Mindlin & Mulvey; Elliott Erwitt/Magnum; Juan Barberis/Melissa Turk & The Artist Network; Mike Yamashita/Woodfin Camp; Francois Gohier/Photo Researchers; © Hank Morgan/VHSID Lab/ECE Dept., University of Massachusetts/Science Source/Photo Researchers.

Library of Congress Catalog Card Number: 87-82741
ISBN: 0-307-70110-7

ABCDEFGHIJK

The letter *J* began with the Egyptian word picture for "hand." It has the same origins as the letter *I*.

The ancient Greeks and Romans wrote the letter the same way. It looked like our capital *I*.

Medieval scribes were the first to give the letter its present form by adding a tail.

Jackson, Andrew

Andrew Jackson was the seventh president of the United States, and the first to come from a poor family. Jackson served as president for two terms, from 1829 to 1837. He was a popular president who believed common people should be given the chance to have better lives.

Jackson was born in 1767 on a small farm near the border of North and South Carolina. He was the son of Irish immigrants. At 13, he left home to fight in the Revolutionary War. He was captured by the British a year later. A British officer handed his boots to Jackson and ordered him to clean them. When Jackson refused, the officer took a sword and cut Jackson's left hand and head. Jackson had these scars for the rest of his life.

After the war, Jackson became a successful lawyer in Tennessee. He also represented that state in Congress. His wife, Rachel Donelson Robards, was from Tennessee.

Andrew Jackson was a war hero and a popular and effective U.S. president.

Jackson served as a general in the Tennessee militia in 1802. In 1812, the United States once again went to war with Great Britain. During this time, the Creek Indians were attacking American settlers near present-day Alabama. In 1814, Jackson and his men killed 800 Creek braves at the Battle of Horseshoe Bend. The Creek Indians were forced to give up a large amount of land. Jackson's leadership and strong will were greatly admired. He was nicknamed "Old Hickory" because soldiers said he was as tough as the wood of a hickory tree.

In 1815, Jackson defeated the British forces at the Battle of New Orleans. This victory, at the end of the War of 1812, made him a national hero. But when he ran for president in 1824, he failed to win. He ran again in 1828. This time he was successful.

The day Jackson took office, 20,000 of his supporters crowded into the White House for a noisy celebration. Jackson rewarded people who had helped him get elected by giving them government jobs. This practice was called the *spoils system.*

Jackson was a strong president. He often argued with Congress and refused to sign their bills into law. He favored the rights of workers and rule by the common people.

Jackson was reelected in 1832. At the end of his second term, he retired to his home in Tennessee, where he died in 1845.

See also **Revolutionary War; Indian Wars;** and **War of 1812.**

Jamaica, *see* West Indies

Jesse James and his gang of outlaws terrified midwestern towns in the 1870s.

James, Jesse

Jesse James is one of the most famous outlaws in United States history. The son of a Baptist minister, Jesse Woodson James was born in Clay County, Missouri, in 1847. He was a young boy when his father died. During the Civil War, James and his brother, Frank, joined a band of Confederate outlaws called Quantrill's Raiders. The group attacked Union forces in two states, Kansas and Missouri. In a single raid on Lawrence, Kansas, in 1863, the band brutally murdered 150 people.

After the Civil War, the two James brothers formed their own gang and began to rob small banks and hold up stagecoaches and trains. In 1873, the James gang tried to rob the First National Bank of Northfield, Minnesota. The whole town banded together to keep the gang from escaping. But the two James brothers got away. After a few years, they started robbing trains again.

Jesse James went into hiding in 1881 after a $5,000 reward was offered for his arrest. He moved with his wife and children to St. Joseph, Missouri, and lived quietly under the name Thomas Howard. James was shot and killed on April 3, 1882, by Robert Ford, a member of his gang who wished to collect the reward money.

Jamestown

Jamestown was the first permanent English settlement in the Americas. It was founded by a group of colonists looking for gold and treasure in the New World. The colonists reached the shores of Virginia in April 1607. They named their settlement after the British king, James I.

The colonists faced many hardships. Half of them were gentlemen who had never done hard work such as building or farming. Jamestown's land was swampy and had many mosquitoes, which carried disease. During the first winter, about a third of the settlers died. Their leader, Captain John Smith, helped save Jamestown. Smith ordered the men to plant crops and stop looking for gold. He asked the Indian chief, Powhatan, to give the settlers corn and meat.

Things got worse in 1609 when Smith was injured and returned to England. Indian attacks, disease, and a shortage of food almost wiped out the colony. About 60 settlers survived the winter. Later, this winter was known as the "starving time."

In spring, new supplies and more settlers arrived. Once the settlers began to grow tobacco and raise families in the colony, its future was secure.

See also **Smith, John.**

Early settlers at Jamestown are building a settlement at the water's edge.

Japan

Capital: Tokyo
Area: 143,750 square miles (372,213 square kilometers)
Population (1985): about 120,731,000
Official language: Japanese

Japan is an island nation off the eastern coast of Asia. Because Japan is so far east, the Japanese see the sun rise before the rest of Asia sees it. That is why Japan is often called the "Land of the Rising Sun." The red circle on the Japanese flag represents the rising sun.

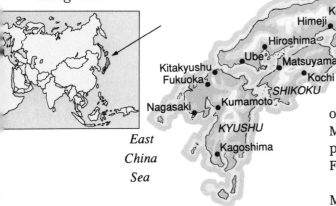

Land Many islands make up the nation of Japan. These islands stretch for more than 1,000 miles (1,610 kilometers) from north to south. Almost all of Japan's people live on the four largest islands—Hokkaido, Honshu, Kyushu, and Shikoku.

As an island nation, Japan has thousands of miles of coastline. That is one reason why fishing is an important part of Japanese life. Japanese fishermen catch more fish each year than the fishermen of any other nation.

Fishing is also important because the land of Japan is very rugged and not good for growing most crops. Three-quarters of the country is covered by mountains and hills. Two important crops that grow well in Japan are tea and rice.

On the island of Honshu, there is a group of volcanoes. One of them is the famous Mount Fuji. On a clear day, people in Japan's capital city, Tokyo, can see Mount Fuji's snowy top.

Japan is in an active earthquake zone. More than 1,000 earthquakes are reported there every year. Most are too small for a person to feel. But large earthquakes have caused serious damage.

People Japan is one of the world's most crowded nations. It has half as many people as the United States, but less land than the state of California.

Most Japanese live in or near the big cities. Tokyo, has more than 8 million people. Osaka, Nagoya, and Yokohama have more than 2 million people each.

Japan is a great industrial power. It produces more goods than any other nation except for the United States and the Soviet Union. Japanese automobiles and electronic products—such as computers, stereos, and televisions—are sold in all parts of the world.

Most of Japan's goods are produced by a few large companies. These companies not only pay the workers' salaries but do things to improve the workers' lives. Workers feel loyal to their company. Many work for the same company from the day they leave school to the day they retire.

Life for many people in Japan is much like life in the United States. They live in modern homes and take automobiles or fast trains to work. American movies and music are popular among Japan's young people.

Still, Japanese traditions remain strong. Some have spread outside Japan. Americans study Japanese *martial arts*—such as karate and judo. These were practiced centuries ago by warriors. Also, Japanese foods have become popular in U.S. cities.

History According to legend, Japan was founded as a nation in the 600s B.C. After A.D. 400, the Yamato family brought all of Japan under one rule.

Much of Japan's early culture came from its neighbors. Its system of writing came from China. The Buddhist religion came from China and Korea. Over centuries, the Japanese made changes in these traditions. Today, Japanese writing is quite different from Chinese. Japanese Buddhism has also become different from the Buddhism practiced in other countries. (*See* **Buddhism.**)

Beginning in the 1100s, groups of warriors battled for control of the country. These warriors called themselves *samurai*. For 700 years, Japan was ruled by samurai leaders called *shoguns*. The samurai had many rules and customs, like the knights of Europe in the Middle Ages.

For hundreds of years, Japan had little contact with other countries. Then in the 1800s, the United States and other nations began trading with Japan. Soon Japan was changing into a strong, modern country. Old traditions and new mixed together.

In the late 1800s and early 1900s, Japan fought in wars against Russia, China, and Korea. Then in the 1930s, Japanese leaders tried to conquer China and other parts of Asia. In 1941, they bombed a U.S. Navy base at Pearl Harbor in Hawaii. The United States, along with other countries, went to war against Japan in World War II.

By 1945, the Japanese were losing the war, but were still fighting. The United States used a new weapon—the atomic bomb—against the Japanese cities of Hiroshima and Nagasaki. A few days later, the Japanese surrendered, and the war was over. (*See* **World War II** and **Hiroshima.**)

After the war, with help from the United States and lots of hard work, Japan became a strong and wealthy nation again.

These Japanese children are using chopsticks to eat their noodles at snacktime.

Jazz may have begun in music for funeral processions like this one in New Orleans.

jazz

Jazz is a kind of music that began in the United States in the late 1800s. It is popular around the world, especially in the United States. Many people think of it as America's special kind of music.

No one knows just how jazz began. But we do know that it grew out of the music of black Americans. The earliest jazz musicians were black, and they used several kinds of black music. They used hymns and spirituals that were sung in black churches. They used work songs—songs that people sang as they worked together in the fields or on the docks.

Early jazz was played for funeral parades. It was also played for happy celebrations. It had a lively "beat" that made it good for dancing. The *stomp, rag,* and *cakewalk* were some of the dances for jazz music.

Jazz could be sad. Jazz singers sang about losing a sweetheart or being out of work. These songs were called *blues.* "Singin' the blues" means feeling sad. The blues used strange, rich harmonies that other music of that time never used. Bessie Smith is one of the best-known blues singers.

Early Jazz Around 1900, black musicians began to gather to play the new music they were inventing. One famous place for early jazz was New Orleans, Louisiana. But soon people were also playing and listening to jazz in Kansas City, Chicago, Baltimore, New York, and other cities.

Most early jazz was played by small bands with four, five, or six instruments. These usually included drums, a string bass or a tuba, a banjo or guitar, a trumpet or trombone, and a clarinet. The drums, bass, and banjo provided the rhythm. The horns and clarinets provided the melodies, playing together or taking turns playing solos.

The players in a jazz band *improvised* —made up their parts as they played. Good jazz musicians knew many tunes and could make up many variations on them. When a player took a solo, it was a chance to show some new and exciting way to play a particular tune. A jazz band never played a song the same way twice.

Louis Armstrong was one of the early jazz trumpeters. Armstrong began playing in New Orleans when he was a teenager. Soon he was playing in bands in Chicago and New York. By the time he died, in 1971, he had played jazz in nearly every part of the world.

Armstrong also sang in a style called *scat.* A scat singer uses the voice like an instrument, singing rhythms and syllables instead of words. Many blues singers add scat to their songs.

Trumpeter Louis Armstrong was one of the giants of early jazz.

Two jazz greats—Benny Goodman on clarinet and Lionel Hampton on vibraphone—
play together as part of a quartet. The other instruments are drums and stringed bass.

Big-Band Jazz In the 1920s, home radio was brand-new, and record players were becoming popular. These two inventions helped spread jazz. Young people liked to go to big dance halls and dance to live bands. By the 1930s, many of the dance bands played a kind of jazz called *swing*. The bandleader Benny Goodman was called the "King of Swing."

These jazz dance bands had as many as 20 or 25 players. One important instrument was the saxophone. Big jazz bands had three kinds of saxophones—alto, tenor, and baritone. The piano and clarinet were important big jazz band instruments, too.

Two of the most famous big bands were those led by Count Basie and Duke Ellington. Count Basie's band started out in Kansas City in the 1920s and played for more than 50 years. Duke Ellington's band first became famous in New York City and then traveled all over the world. Ellington wrote many new compositions for his band. He played in concert halls as well as dance halls. (*See* **Ellington, Duke.**)

Jazz singers often sang with the bands. Like the players, the singers improvised. Billie Holiday and Ella Fitzgerald were two of the best-loved jazz singers.

Modern Jazz In the 1950s, jazz became less popular for dancing. Instead, quartets and other small groups began experimenting with new sounds. The new kinds of jazz took many names. Charlie Parker, a saxophone player, played *bop*. Miles Davis, a trumpet player, played *cool jazz*. Musicians mixed jazz with Caribbean and classical music. Others mixed it with rock 'n' roll. (*See* **rock music.**)

Today, many people follow jazz. They play or listen to jazz in nightclubs and concert halls. They collect jazz records of the past and the present.

At the same time, jazz is everywhere. Many favorite American tunes from musicals and movies, and many favorite performers, use jazz. The sounds of jazz—the beat and the harmonies—are the music that many Americans know best.

See also **music** and **musical instrument.**

Jefferson, Thomas

Thomas Jefferson was the third president of the United States and the author of the Declaration of Independence. He was a great thinker whose ideas helped shape the United States Constitution and the way the government runs. He also studied science, played the violin, and invented some useful things. He helped start the University of Virginia and designed its buildings. He also designed the Virginia Capitol and his own house, Monticello. (*See* **Monticello.**)

Jefferson was born in Albemarle County, Virginia, in April 1743. His father was a wealthy landowner, and his mother came from an old Virginia family. As a boy, Jefferson studied history, literature, Greek, Latin, French, Spanish, and Italian. At age 16, he went to Virginia's College of William and Mary to study mathematics, science, and law. He became a lawyer at age 24.

In 1769, Jefferson was elected to the Virginia legislature. He represented Virginia at the Second Continental Congress, which met to discuss the colonies' problems with Britain. In 1776, the Congress decided to declare the colonies free of Great Britain. Jefferson was asked to write a statement explaining why. He took a little over two weeks to write the Declaration of Independence. (*See* **Declaration of Independence.**)

Jefferson returned to Virginia politics. He helped change the laws so more people could own land and vote. He also made a plan for free public education. Jefferson was governor of Virginia during the Revolutionary War.

Jefferson became minister to France in 1784. President George Washington made him secretary of state in 1789. Jefferson approved of the new Constitution, signed in 1789. But he wanted it to have a statement that protected individual rights. He made sure his ideas went into the Bill of Rights, completed in 1791. (*See* **Bill of Rights.**)

Jefferson was elected vice president in 1796, and president in 1800 and 1804. During his two presidencies, he tried to run a fair and honest government. He also got Congress to agree to the Louisiana Purchase. (*See* **Louisiana Purchase.**)

After his second term, Jefferson retired to Monticello, his home in Virginia. He worked on his inventions, music, farming, and writing. He died on July 4, 1826, 50 years after the Declaration of Independence was signed.

See also **Revolutionary War.**

Thomas Jefferson had many interests. He was an architect, inventor, and musician. He wrote the Declaration of Independence and served eight years as U.S. president.

jellyfish

The jellyfish is an animal that lives in the sea. It looks like an umbrella made of jelly. Long *tentacles* hang like strings from the body. The tentacles are lined with stinging cells. Within each stinging cell is a long, coiled thread with a barb on its end. When a fish or other sea animal touches the tentacles, the threads shoot out of the stinging cells. The barbs pierce the fish's skin and inject a poison. The poison kills the fish. Then the tentacles carry the fish to the jellyfish's mouth.

The jellyfish below is eating a small fish. At right, a tiny fish hides under the bell of a jellyfish for protection.

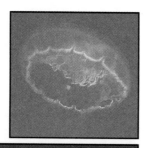

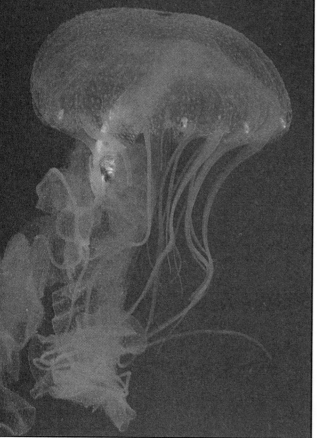

Jellyfish are not fish. Fish are *vertebrates*—animals with backbones. Jellyfish are *invertebrates*—animals without backbones. Jellyfish are related to corals, sea anemones, and other sea animals that have stinging cells. (*See* **coral** and **sea anemone.**)

There are about 200 kinds of jellyfish. They are found in all the oceans of the world. Most are small. But the giant jellyfish may weigh almost a ton. Its huge body may be 2.5 meters (8 feet) wide. Its tentacles may be longer than 50 meters (165 feet).

Jellyfish are poor swimmers. They drift with the ocean waves and currents. During a storm, many may be tossed onto the shore.

Jenner, Edward

Edward Jenner was an English doctor born in 1749. He discovered a way to keep people safe from a dangerous disease. His discovery—*vaccination*—was one of the most important in the history of medicine.

In Jenner's time, smallpox was a terrible disease that killed thousands each year. A milder disease called cowpox sometimes infected people who lived near cows. It made people sick for a short time, but hardly ever caused death. Jenner learned that people who once had cowpox seemed *immune* to smallpox. Even if members of their families got smallpox, they would not get it.

In 1796, Jenner took material from a cowpox sore and put it on the arm of an eight-year-old boy. The boy got cowpox, but soon recovered. Six weeks later, Jenner took material from a smallpox sore and put it on the boy's arm. The boy did not get smallpox.

Jenner spent the rest of his life telling others about vaccination. At first, many people thought Jenner's ideas were evil. But thousands of people were vaccinated. As a result, there have been no cases of smallpox in the whole world since 1977.

Vaccines now exist for many other diseases. We remember Edward Jenner not only because he found an effective way to protect people from smallpox, but because

In Jerusalem, the Wailing Wall (bottom) is sacred to Jews. The Omar Mosque (with gold dome) is sacred to Muslims. Jerusalem is also a holy place to Christians.

he worked so hard to spread the practice of vaccination.

See also **vaccine.**

Jerusalem

Jerusalem is the capital city of Israel, in the Middle East. To the people of three world religions, Jerusalem is a holy city. Some of the most important events in Judaism, Christianity, and Islam happened in Jerusalem.

About 1,000 years before Jesus was born, the ancient kingdom of Israel made Jerusalem its capital. King Solomon built a temple there for worshiping God. It was the holiest place for the Jews. Enemies destroyed the temple, but the Jews built it again. Much later, in A.D. 70, the Romans destroyed the second temple. The Jews scattered to many parts of the world. Today, the only part of the ancient temple that is still standing is called the Wailing Wall. Jews from all over the world come to the Wailing Wall to pray.

About 40 years before the second temple was destroyed, a Jewish teacher named Jesus taught in Jerusalem. The city's rulers feared Jesus' teachings and had him put to death. But his followers formed the Christian Church. Today, the Church of the Holy Sepulchre stands where Jesus was killed. Thousands of Christians visit Jerusalem every year. (*See* **Jesus.**)

About 600 years later, the prophet Muhammad started the Islamic religion. Muslims—the followers of Islam—believe that Muhammad rose into heaven from a spot in Jerusalem. A mosque called the Dome of the Rock was built on that spot. It is one of the holiest places to Muslims.

Jerusalem has had a violent history. It has been conquered, destroyed, and rebuilt many times. Muslims ruled it from the 600s to the 1000s. Then Christian Crusaders from Europe came to take it away. Finally, in 1099, they succeeded. But less than 100 years later, the Muslims won back the city.

Fighting over Jerusalem continued into recent years. In 1948, the Jewish nation of Israel was set up west of Jerusalem. Part of the city belonged to Israel. Part belonged to Jordan, a Muslim country to the east. Israelis believed that all of Jerusalem should be under one government. Israel captured the Jordanian part of Jerusalem. Today, all of Jerusalem is under Israel's control.

The city's oldest district—called Old City —is much like a city of many centuries ago. Most of the holy places are there. The New City has modern apartments, factories, and office buildings. The Israeli government has its offices there. Most people in Jerusalem are Jewish, but Arabs also live there.

See also **Israel; Judaism; Christianity; Islam;** and **Crusades.**

11

Jesus

Jesus Christ began the Christian religion about 2,000 years ago. Christians believe Jesus is the son of God, who came to earth to save all mankind. The teachings of Jesus have influenced literature, art, and even governments. Today, Christianity is the world's largest religion, with over 1 billion followers.

The story of Jesus is told in the *New Testament* of the Christian Bible. The first four books of the New Testament are the Gospels of Matthew, Mark, Luke, and John. The word *gospel* means "good news." The Gospels tell about the life and teachings of Jesus. The Acts of the Apostles tell what happened in the years following his death.

Birth of Jesus Jesus' mother was a young woman named Mary. According to the Gospels, a messenger from God told Mary that she would have a baby who would be the son of God. She was told to name the child Jesus, which means "savior" in Hebrew. Mary and her husband, Joseph, were to raise the child as their own.

Mary and Joseph lived in Nazareth, a town located in an area of the Middle East known as Palestine. Palestine today is part of the country of Israel. Before Jesus was born, Mary and Joseph had to leave Nazareth and travel to the town of Bethlehem. All the inns were filled, and they found no place to stay the night. So they took shelter in a stable with farm animals. It was here that Jesus was born.

Life of Jesus Jesus grew up in Nazareth. Joseph was a carpenter, and Jesus probably learned to use the tools in Joseph's workshop. Jesus read Hebrew and worshiped with his family at the temple.

When he was about 30 years old, Jesus left Nazareth and began to travel through the villages and towns of Galilee, in northern Palestine. He believed he had been sent by God to bring people a message.

Jesus told people that God loved them the way parents love their children. He said God wanted all His children to love and respect

According to the Bible, Jesus fed a crowd with a few fishes and a few loaves of bread.

each other and to love Him in return.

Jesus chose 12 followers to help him with his work. Their leader was a man named Peter. After Jesus' death, these men, the *apostles*, became the first leaders of the new Christian community. (*See* **Peter.**)

Peter and the other apostles believed that Jesus was the *Messiah* promised by God to the Jews. Jews believed that the Messiah would be sent by God to save and unite his chosen people. Jesus' followers, however, believed that Jesus came to save not only Jews but all people. (*See* **Paul.**)

Jesus liked to help poor people and people in trouble. Some people did not trust Jesus because he treated everyone the same way. Jesus answered that God loved everyone, but especially those who needed Him the most. The Gospels tell of Jesus performing amazing miracles. They say he brought a dead man back to life and touched the eyes of the blind to make them see. Jesus often told *parables*—short stories that teach a lesson—in order to get his message across to people.

Death of Jesus Jesus became very popular among the people of Palestine. This made other religious leaders jealous. It also frightened the Roman rulers of Palestine. They were afraid that Jesus would someday lead a revolt against them. Jesus' enemies had him arrested one night in Jerusalem during the Jewish feast of *Passover.* Jesus was in a garden praying when the Roman soldiers came to get him. They knew where to find him because he had been betrayed by one of his own chosen followers, Judas Iscariot.

Just before his arrest, Jesus ate the Passover meal with his chosen followers. He knew that he was going to die soon. He told his followers to remember him by eating bread and drinking wine together, just as they were doing that night. Christians call this event the *Last Supper.*

The Roman governor of Palestine, Pontius Pilate, sentenced Jesus to be *crucified*—to die on a cross. Christians say that three days after his death, Jesus came back to life again. This is called his *resurrection.* Jesus spent the next 40 days teaching his followers. He then rose into heaven. This is called his *ascension.*

Throughout the year, Christians recall the major events in the life of Jesus. *Christmas* celebrates his birth. His death is remembered on *Good Friday,* and his resurrection on *Easter Sunday.* At *communion* services, Christians act out the Last Supper by eating bread and drinking wine as Jesus told his apostles to do.

jet engine

The air you blow into a toy balloon is *compressed.* Compressed air is a lot of air that has been forced into a small space under pressure. The compressed air pushes against the inside of the balloon and makes it stretch. If you let go of the balloon without tying the stem, the compressed air escapes at high speed. It sends the balloon speeding in the opposite direction like a small jet.

A jet engine works much like a speeding balloon. The engine produces *thrust*—pushing power—by releasing gas under great pressure. Some jet planes travel faster than the speed of sound.

From the outside, a jet engine looks like a smooth, hollow tube, up to 6 meters (20 feet) long or longer. It is open at both ends. The jet engine's moving parts are inside.

Huge sets of fans, called *turbines,* are the main parts of a jet engine. The first set of

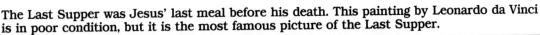

The Last Supper was Jesus' last meal before his death. This painting by Leonardo da Vinci is in poor condition, but it is the most famous picture of the Last Supper.

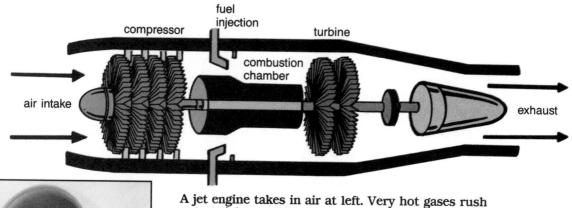

air intake

compressor

fuel
injection

combustion
chamber

turbine

exhaust

A jet engine takes in air at left. Very hot gases rush out at right, pushing the jet to the left.

Above, a jet intake shows the turbines. Below, a plane with jets on each wing and on the tail.

turbines makes up the *turbocompressor*. As the blades of the turbocompressor spin, they suck in air through the opening at the front of the engine. As all this air is forced into narrow tubes, it is compressed and becomes very hot.

The very hot, compressed air enters a chamber, called the *combustion chamber*, in the middle of the jet engine. Here, jet fuel is sprayed into the extremely hot, compressed air. The heat ignites the fuel, producing even hotter gases and high pressure. The hot gases expand and have nowhere to go but backward, toward the exhaust nozzles at the rear of the engine.

Before the exhaust gases can escape, another set of turbines forces them into a chamber called the *afterburner*. Here, any traces of unburned jet fuel are burned at temperatures of over 1,600° C (3,000° F). This makes the gases in the afterburner expand even more. When the exhaust gases finally escape through the rear nozzles, they have tremendous force.

Frank Whittle, of England, is given credit for inventing the jet engine in 1930. Without the work of Whittle and others who perfected the jet engine, we might still be using only propeller-driven aircraft.

See also **engine.**

jet stream

Jet streams are rivers of fast-moving air high above the earth. Most jet streams form in the *troposphere,* the lowest layer of the atmosphere. Others develop higher up, in the *stratosphere.* A jet stream may be thousands of miles long, hundreds of miles wide, and thousands of feet thick. Jet stream winds range in speed from 80 to 560 kilometers per hour (50 to 350 miles per hour). The fastest winds are in the center. The slowest ones are on the edges of the current. Like other winds, jet streams are caused by large differences in temperature and air pressure between air masses. (*See* **atmosphere; weather;** and **wind.**)

Most jet streams exist year round. They flow from west to east, following the earth's rotation. They have a winding and changing path around the planet. The polar jet streams circle above the North and South poles. The subtropical jet streams flow above the areas between the poles and the equator. Jet streams above the equator blow only in the summer. Instead of flowing from west to east, they flow east to west—from Southeast Asia toward Africa.

In summer, jet streams move away from the equator. They take warm air with them. In winter, they move away from the poles, taking along cold air. The winds of jet streams are weaker in summer than winter. (*See* **climate.**)

Jet streams may shift daily, causing changes in weather patterns. In the United States, when a polar jet stream moves far south, a cold wave results. When a jet stream shifts north, a heat wave occurs. Jet streams also influence how storms begin. Scientists are studying this and other effects of jet streams on weather.

Jet streams were not closely studied until World War II. American bomber pilots flying west over Japan were slowed down by strong winds blowing east. When this happened, the pilots feared running out of fuel. Instead of completing their mission, they dropped their bombs into the sea and returned home.

Today, pilots flying from west to east try to fly in a jet stream that will push them along faster. Those flying west avoid jet streams to keep from being delayed.

jewelry

Jewelry includes such things as necklaces, pins, rings, bracelets, earrings, and other ornaments that people wear. Most of the fine jewelry we are familiar with is made of precious metals and gems. Gold, silver, platinum, and copper are some metals used in jewelry. Diamonds, rubies, emeralds, and sapphires are some precious gems. Other

The jet stream blows from west to east around the world (bottom). It brings changes in weather and also affects flight times—flying west is slower than flying east.

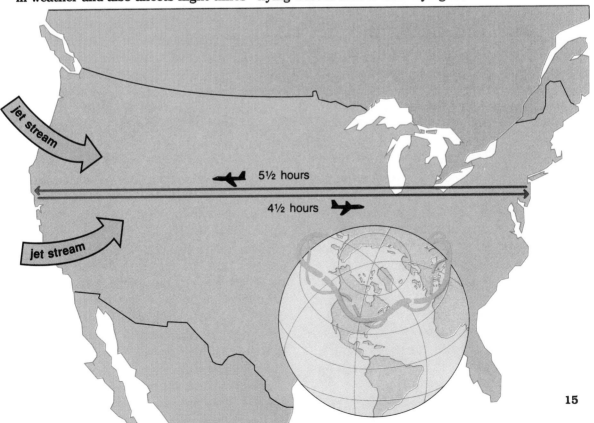

jet stream

jet stream

5½ hours

4½ hours

Jewelry has been popular in many times and places.
At right, a girl tries on inexpensive jewelry.

gems—such as jade, turquoise, garnets, and topaz—are often used. Ivory, pearls, and amber, which come from animals, are also made into jewelry.

Humans probably have worn ornaments since very early times. They used feathers, shells, and bones before they learned how to work with metals. Later, many people used metals and gems because they are beautiful and last much longer than feathers, shells, or bones.

The earliest known gold jewelry comes from ancient Egypt. Egyptians wore jewelry in their hair, around their necks and waists, in their ears, and on their fingers as rings. They set uncut stones into metal. The ancient Greeks knew how to work gold into fine designs. They also made cameos. These were simple carvings, often of faces, made out of shells.

The Chinese used jade, ivory, and gold in jewelry. The Indians of South America made beautiful jewelry of gold. North American Indians made jewelry of silver and shells and stones.

People have admired jewelry for its beauty and its value. Jewelry can also be a symbol. In many places, if you wore jewelry, everyone knew you were important or rich. The crown of a king or queen is a piece of jewelry that symbolizes special power. Jewelry may also have religious meanings.

Jewelry can have practical uses. Watches tell time, but they may be jewelry, too. Fancy buttons and clasps help hold clothing together. (*See* **button.**)

People wear jewelry in different ways. In Asia or Africa, women may wear a stone or other jewel on one side of their noses or attached to their lips. They may think it strange that women in Europe or the Americas wear earrings.

Many people wear *costume jewelry.* Costume jewelry may be beautiful, but it is not made of precious metals and gems. It may be made of plastic or inexpensive metal. It may be set with imitation gems. Costume jewelry is less expensive than precious jewelry, so more people can afford it.

See also **gold; silver; platinum;** and **gem.**

16

Joan of Arc

Joan of Arc was a French peasant who became the national heroine of France and a saint of the Roman Catholic Church.

Joan was born around 1412. France and England were fighting the Hundred Years' War for control of French land. When Joan was in her teens, she said she heard voices telling her that with her help French king Charles VII could defeat the English. She went to the king and persuaded him that her powers came from heaven. He put her in command of his troops.

Dressed in armor, Joan led her troops to victory at Orléans in 1429. From then on, she was known as the Maid of Orléans. She won four more battles, even though she was wounded twice. Later, she stood beside Charles as he was officially crowned.

Charles asked Joan to keep fighting the English. She was captured in 1430 and put on trial as a witch. English churchmen said the "voices" she heard came from the devil.

Joan was burned at the stake in 1431. Her life and death did much to unite the French and drive the English out of France.

Johnson, Andrew, *see* presidents of the U.S.

Johnson, Lyndon B.

Lyndon Baines Johnson was the 36th president of the United States, from 1963 to 1969. He was a powerful leader who worked hard for civil rights and to help the poor.

Johnson was born in Stonewall, Texas, in 1908. His family was poor, but he was determined to succeed. He graduated from high school when he was only 15, and then he worked his way through college. He was elected to Congress in 1937, and became a U.S. senator from Texas in 1948. In 1960, when John F. Kennedy was elected president, Johnson became vice president. When Kennedy was killed in Dallas, Texas, in 1963, Johnson was sworn in as president. In 1964, he was elected to a full term as president.

Johnson's "War on Poverty" created new jobs for the poor. His other programs improved schools and cities. But his handling of the Vietnam War was not popular. Johnson tried to win the war by sending more U.S. soldiers and supplies. This caused bitter arguments, because many people felt all U.S. troops should come home. In an attempt to unite the country, Johnson decided not to run for president in 1968. He died in Texas in 1973.

See also **Vietnam War.**

President Lyndon B. Johnson greets supporters at an airport during a visit in 1966.

John the Baptist

John the Baptist was a Jewish teacher and prophet. He lived about 2,000 years ago in the land of *Palestine,* which today is part of the country of Israel. His story is told in the New Testament of the Christian Bible. (*See* **Bible.**)

John was a cousin of Jesus Christ. He announced the coming of Jesus and prepared the way by telling people to turn away from sin and lead better lives. He *baptized* those who accepted his message by having them step into the Jordan River. The ceremony of baptism was a symbol of a person's wish to start a new life.

Before Jesus began preaching, he went to John and asked to be baptized. John felt unworthy to do this. He believed that Jesus was the *messiah*—the one chosen by God to save all people. He agreed to baptize Jesus only after Jesus told him it was God's will that he do so.

John was sent to prison when he criticized Herod Antipas, the ruler of Palestine. John was put to death at the request of Salome, Herod's stepdaughter.

See also **Jesus.**

John the Evangelist

John the Evangelist was a fisherman who became a follower of Jesus Christ. John and his brother, James, were in a boat fixing their nets when Jesus first talked to them. The two brothers stopped what they were doing and joined him. John and James became two of the 12 men chosen by Jesus to follow him.

John, James, and Peter were the three followers Jesus relied on the most. They were with Jesus in the garden of Gethsemane when he was arrested by Roman soldiers. During Jesus' trial and when Jesus was dying, Peter and James were frightened and tried to keep out of sight. Only John remained a faithful friend to Jesus until the very end of Jesus' life. (*See* **Peter.**)

John went with Jesus to the hill where Jesus was *crucified*—nailed to a wooden cross and left to die. John stood with Mary, the mother of Jesus, as Jesus was dying. Jesus asked John to take care of Mary after he died.

John became a leader of the Christian community. People believe he wrote the Gospel of John, the fourth book of the New Testament of the Christian Bible. They also believe he wrote the Book of the Revelation, the last book in the New Testament.

See also **Jesus** and **Bible.**

joint

The place where two bones meet is called a joint. Movable joints allow the body to bend, twist, and turn. If we did not have movable joints between our bones, we would not be able to move at all. Our legs and feet, arms and hands, back and neck—even our jaws —would be locked.

In most joints, the ends of the bones are covered with a layer of cartilage. It keeps the bones from rubbing against one another and allows easy movement. The joint is covered by a tough sleeve. The inside of the sleeve produces a slippery fluid. When the ends of the bones rub against each other, this slippery fluid acts just like oil in a machine. It

The hip joint is a ball-and-socket joint that allows movement in many directions.

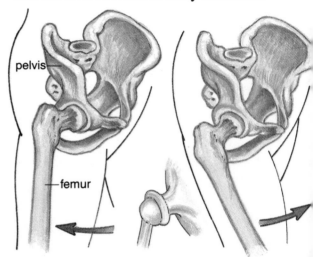

pelvis

femur

further reduces the rubbing between the moving parts of the joint.

The two bones that make up a joint are held together by tough elastic fibers called *ligaments.* These ligaments stretch as the joint moves. They let the joint move far enough, but not too far.

There are several kinds of movable joints. Shoulders and hips have *ball-and-socket joints.* The head of one bone is shaped like a round ball. It fits into the cup-shaped socket of another bone.

Hinge joints allow movement forward and backward, like a door on a hinge. You have hinge joints in your elbows and between your finger bones. The joints at the knees and knuckles are like hinge joints, but they also allow some movement from side to side.

Pivot joints allow a turning movement. Pivot joints in your neck allow you to turn your head from side to side.

A *fibrous joint* holds bones together with tough fibers that are not really movable. Joints of this kind are found between the bones of the skull. Some other joints are held together with cartilage. They allow only a little movement. Joints of this kind connect the individual bones of the backbone.

Sometimes, joints can be injured. When you suddenly bend or twist a joint too far, you cause a *sprain.* The ligaments that hold

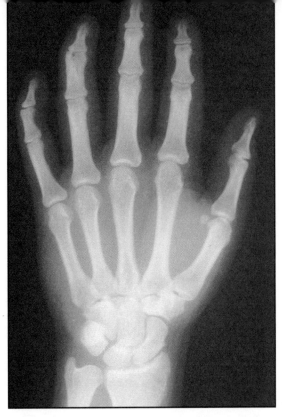

An X ray of a hand shows that each finger has three joints and the thumb has two.

the joint together have been stretched or torn. A *dislocation* is more serious. The ends of the bones are moved out of place at the joint. Any injury that affects a joint should be examined by a doctor.

Arthritis is swelling of the joints. There are several kinds of arthritis. All cause pain and stiffness in the joints. Many people have some arthritis as they get older.

The elbow joint is a hinge. It allows movement in fewer directions.

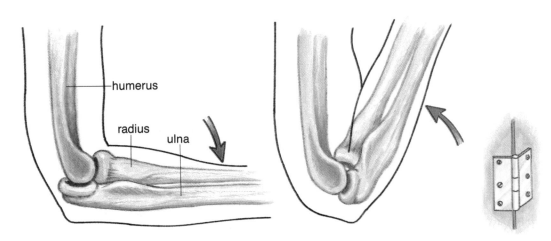

humerus

radius

ulna

What does the mayonnaise say
when you look in the refrigerator?

"Shut the door — I'm dressing!"

What has four wheels and flies?

A garbage truck.

joke

A joke is a funny thing a person says or does. Some jokes are silly stories. Other jokes ask questions that have silly answers. Still other jokes are not in words but in funny actions.

People like to tell jokes to make others laugh. People have different ideas about what is funny, but everyone likes to laugh.

Some jokes use words that sound alike. One famous joke is "What is black and white and red all over?" The answer is "A newspaper. It is black and white and *read* all over." (*Red* and *read* sound alike.)

Other jokes use words that can have different meanings. "Why did the fool throw the clock out of the window?" The answer is "Because he wanted to see time fly."

Jokes do not always need words. Most people think it is funny to see 20 circus clowns riding in one tiny car!

Practical jokes are jokes people play on others. Many April Fools' tricks are practical jokes. But some practical jokes are mean or dangerous. They are not funny to the person the joke is played on. The best jokes make everybody laugh. The worst jokes hurt someone's feelings.

See also **April Fools' Day.**

Jolliet, Louis

Louis Jolliet was a French Canadian who explored the Mississippi River in 1673. He traveled with a French missionary, Jacques Marquette. The two were among the first white explorers to see the upper part of the Mississippi River.

Jolliet was born in Quebec in 1645. As a young man, he explored the area around the Great Lakes. Later, the governor of Canada asked Jolliet to trace the course of a great river. The Indians called this river the Mississippi. The governor hoped the river would be a good trade route to the Far East.

Jolliet, Marquette, and five others set out by canoe from Lake Michigan. They paddled through Green Bay to the Fox River. Then they carried their canoes to the Wisconsin River. They paddled down the Wisconsin until they reached the Mississippi, then south as far as the Arkansas River. They returned home after realizing that the Mississippi flowed into the Gulf of Mexico, near Spanish settlements.

Jolliet drew maps of the trip, which covered 2,500 miles (4,000 kilometers). The French government honored him by giving him an island in the Gulf of St. Lawrence.

See also **Marquette, Jacques** and **Mississippi River.**

Louis Jolliet explored from Lake Michigan to the lower Mississippi River.

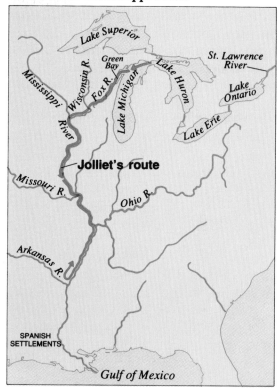

John Paul Jones commanded an American ship in the Revolutionary War. When a British captain wanted him to surrender, Jones said, "Sir, I have not yet begun to fight!"

Jones, John Paul

John Paul Jones was a naval hero of the Revolutionary War. He is known today as the "Father of the United States Navy."

Jones's real name was simply John Paul. He was born in Scotland in 1747 and went to sea at the age of 12. On board ship, the small, thin Scotsman quickly learned how to sail. Soon, he was able to *navigate*—control the ship's course by using the stars as guides. By age 21, John Paul had become a sea captain. He was very strict with his crew, and harshly punished those who did not follow his orders. This led some of his crew to *mutiny*—rise up against him—in 1773. A crewman was killed during the mutiny, and Paul was accused of murder. Paul fled to America to avoid trial. There, he took the last name of Jones to disguise himself.

John Paul Jones joined the new American navy at the beginning of the Revolutionary War. He served on the first ship to fly the young nation's flag. In 1777, the Continental Congress gave Jones command of a new ship, the *Ranger.* Jones sailed the *Ranger* to Great Britain and raided British ports and ships. He also captured the *Drake,* the first British ship seized by the American navy.

In 1779, Jones was put in charge of an old, slow ship. The ship was called the *Bonhomme Richard.* It was named in honor of the American statesman and inventor Benjamin Franklin, who wrote *Poor Richard's Almanack.*

On September 23, 1779, Jones attacked the *Serapis,* a British ship much larger than his own. For three and a half hours, the two ships fought side by side off the eastern coast of Britain. Seeing that the *Bonhomme Richard* was near sinking, the British captain shouted over to Jones, "Are you ready to surrender?" Jones is said to have replied, "Sir, I have not yet begun to fight!" The Americans went on to win the battle. After the British surrendered, Jones and his crew scrambled on board the *Serapis.* The *Bonhomme Richard* sank beneath the waves.

Congress honored John Paul Jones with a gold medal, but no longer needed a navy.

Jones then served in the Russian navy. He died in 1792 and is buried at the U.S. Naval Academy.

See also **Revolutionary War.**

Jordan, *see* Middle East

Juárez, Benito

Benito Juárez (HWAH-rez) is one of Mexico's greatest national heroes. He was president of Mexico when Mexico was struggling to become strong. He was an honest man who tried to help the poor.

Juárez was born in 1806 in Oaxaca, a state in southern Mexico. He was a Zapotec Indian, but learned to speak Spanish. He became a lawyer, hoping to help the Indians and the poor. He was elected governor of Oaxaca in 1848 and tried to make more land available to the poor. Mexico's ruler, General Santa Anna, forced Juárez to leave in 1853. Juárez returned two years later and became Mexico's minister of justice. He was elected president of Mexico in 1861.

At this time, Mexico owed money to European nations. But the treasury was empty,

Benito Juárez is a national hero in Mexico. He was president of Mexico in the 1860s.

and Juárez had to announce that all payments would be stopped for two years. France used this as an excuse to send an Austrian prince, Maximilian, to take over Mexico. With the help of the United States, Juárez forced the French out of Mexico in 1866. Maximilian was captured and killed in 1867.

Juárez then started to work for religious freedom, fair elections, and free education. He died in 1872.

See also **Mexico.**

Judaism

Judaism is one of the world's oldest religions. Its name comes from *Judah,* the southern half of the ancient kingdom of Israel. The people who lived in Israel were known as *Jews.* Judaism was the first religion to state belief in one God. The Christian and Islamic religions both developed from Judaism.

History Jews believe that about 5,000 years ago, God made a *covenant*—an agreement—with their ancestor, Abraham. God promised to bless Abraham and his children if they obeyed and were faithful to him. For this reason, Jews are often called the "chosen people." God repeated this promise to Abraham's son, Isaac, and to Isaac's son, Jacob. Jacob was also known by the name Israel. His descendants came to be called the *children of Israel,* or *Israelites.* (*See* **Israelites** and **Abraham.**)

The Jews lived in the land of Canaan for many years. Today, Canaan is part of the country of Israel. Jacob's son, Joseph, led the Jews out of Canaan and into Egypt when they were threatened by starvation. The Jews lived happily in Egypt until the pharaoh—Egyptian king—made them slaves. God then commanded the Jewish leader Moses to take his people out of Egypt. The flight of the Jews from Egypt back to Canaan is called the *Exodus.*

Back in Canaan, the Jews were organized into 12 tribes. Eventually, they united under

Above, a cantor chants a prayer in a Jewish temple.
Right, symbols of Judaism—the Star of David and
the Torah.

one king, Saul, and formed the kingdom of Israel. The next king, David, helped Israel become powerful and made Jerusalem its capital. His son, Solomon, built a great temple there to honor God.

Israel, however, was surrounded by more powerful nations. It could not defend itself against invasion. In 586 B.C., the Babylonian king, Nebuchadnezzar, destroyed the temple and took many Jews to Babylon. They later returned to Israel and rebuilt the temple. But it was destroyed again in 70 A.D., this time by the Romans.

It was hard for the Jews to live under Roman rule. Jews began to wander throughout the world in search of new homes. This movement is called the *Diaspora*. The Jews were a minority in Christian Europe and were often *persecuted*—made to suffer for their beliefs. Jews were forced to leave England in 1290, and Spain in 1492.

The most terrible moment in Jewish history came in the 1940s, during World War II. In Germany, Adolf Hitler and his followers, the Nazis, tried to kill all the Jews in Europe. More than 6 million Jewish men, women, and children were put to death. This horrible event is called the *Holocaust*. (*See* **Hitler, Adolf**.)

Beliefs and Writings Judaism's most important writings are found in the *Torah* and the *Talmud*. The Torah is made up of the first five books of the Jewish Bible. It tells the story of the Jewish people up until the death of Moses. The basic laws of Judaism are also found in the Torah. The Talmud is a collection of laws that Jews are supposed to follow in order to live a good life. It also describes Jewish customs and relates Jewish folk tales.

According to Jewish belief, God will someday send a *messiah*—a leader who will unite them and defeat their enemies.

Judaism is divided into three groups. *Orthodox* Jews believe that the laws of the Torah and the Talmud were given to Moses by God. They strictly observe all of the traditional Jewish customs and laws. *Reform* Jews think that the laws of the Talmud were written by people and not handed down by

23

Left, after his *bar mitzvah*, a boy holds the sacred scrolls containing the Torah.
Right, a large family celebrates Passover at a *seder*—a special meal.

God. Because of this, they follow the Torah more closely and often do not observe the traditional customs. *Conservative* Jews follow both the Torah and the Talmud, but they combine these ancient writings with modern customs.

Holy Days The *Sabbath*—the seventh day of the week—is a day of rest and worship. For Jews, the Sabbath begins at sunset every Friday and ends at sunset on Saturday. Traditionally, on Friday night, Jews meet for prayer in their temples and then gather at home for the family meal. The mother of the family lights the Sabbath candles. The father says a blessing over a cup of wine.

The temples where Jews worship are called *synagogues*. This is a Greek word that means "house of assembly." Every synagogue has a copy of the Torah, written on parchment and covered with beautiful cloth and silver. It is kept in a chest called the *holy ark*. A light always burns above the ark as a symbol of God's presence in the synagogue. On the Sabbath, a part of the Torah is read by a man from the congregation. Worship

services are led by a *rabbi*, who has studied Jewish law and helps people with their problems.

Rosh Hashanah, the Jewish New Year, is celebrated in the fall. On Rosh Hashanah, people are called to prayer by a great trumpet called a *shofar*, made from a ram's horn.

The ten days beginning with Rosh Hashanah are called the *High Holy Days*. This period ends with *Yom Kippur*, which is the most important of all Jewish holy days. On Yom Kippur, Jews fast during the day. They spend all day in the synagogue asking God for forgiveness. The harvest celebration of *Sukkoth* comes five days later. During this holiday, some Jews build little huts, called *sukkahs*, outside their houses. These remind them of the huts their ancestors lived in during the flight from Egypt. (*See* **Yom Kippur**.)

Hanukkah—"Festival of Lights"—usually comes in December, and lasts eight days. During Hanukkah, people remember how Jewish heroes defeated the Syrians, who tried to make them give up their religion.

Each night during Hanukkah, Jews light one of the candles in a *menorah*—a special candle holder. (*See* **Hanukkah.**)

Purim is a springtime holiday that recalls the story of Esther. Esther was a Jewish heroine who saved the Jews of Persia (now Iran) from people who were planning to kill them.

The feast of *Passover* celebrates the Exodus of the Jews from Egypt. A special meal called a *seder* is served at home. During the seder, prayers are read and all the foods are eaten in a careful order. Each of the foods has a special meaning. For example, *matzoh* is eaten instead of bread. Matzoh bakes very quickly. This reminds the people of how quickly the Jews had to get ready to flee from Egypt. A bitter herb, usually horseradish, symbolizes the bitterness of slavery. (*See* **Passover.**)

Religious ceremonies also take place at important times in a Jew's life. Eight days after a boy is born, he is welcomed into the Jewish faith at a ceremony known as a *bris.* When a boy is 13, he enters the adult Jewish community at a ceremony called a *bar mitzvah.* For girls, there is a similar ceremony called a *bas mitzvah.* At a Jewish marriage ceremony, the bride and groom stand under a tent called a *huppah.* After they make their promises to each other, the groom smashes a wineglass under his shoe. He does this as a reminder of the destruction of Solomon's temple.

Today, there are almost 17 million Jews living throughout the world. The spiritual center for all Jews, however, is the nation of Israel—the land of their ancestors.

See also **Israel.**

jungle

A jungle is a place where tropical plants grow in a tangle. You may think of the rain forests of Africa or South America as jungles. You may imagine monkeys swinging through high branches, or leopards crouched and waiting to jump on their prey. But when scientists speak of a jungle, they usually mean a small, damaged area of a rain forest, where there are no tall trees. New shrubs and young trees are beginning to grow again. Mosses may grow in thick mats on the ground and around tree trunks. The low-growing plants may be so thick that it is difficult to get through them.

Jungles of this kind are temporary. As time passes, this bit of landscape will change. Only the hardiest trees, vines and shrubs will live. Eventually, tall trees will block out sunlight. Many smaller plants will disappear. The area will once again look like the rest of the rain forest.

See also **rain forest.**

When trees in a rain forest are cut down, new plants become a jungle. They grow in so thickly that people cannot pass through.

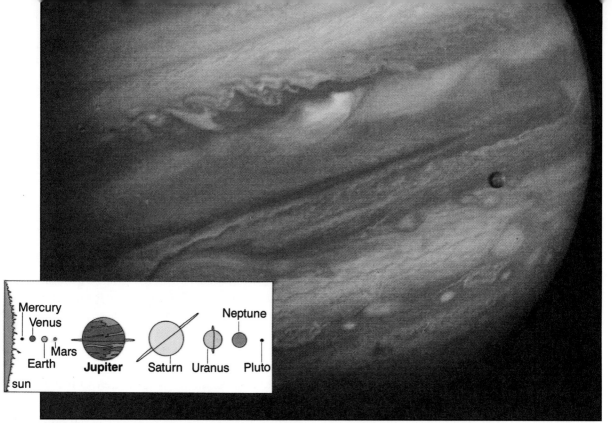

Jupiter, the largest planet in the solar system, as it was photographed by the *Voyager 1* satellite. One of Jupiter's moons is at lower right.

Jupiter

Jupiter is the largest planet in our solar system and the fifth planet out from the sun. If you had a scale to weigh the planets, Jupiter would weigh two and one-half times more than all the other planets combined. Jupiter's diameter is 142,800 kilometers (88,700 miles)—11 times more than Earth's diameter. Jupiter's gravity is about two and one-half times stronger than Earth's.

A year takes a long time on Jupiter. The planet orbits the sun at an average distance of 778 million kilometers (483 million miles). One year on Jupiter—one trip around the sun—takes almost 12 Earth years. But Jupiter spins much faster than Earth does. On Jupiter, a day lasts only about ten hours.

Jupiter's unusual features include a system of rings, and 16 moons. The rings are something like those around the planet Saturn, but fainter. The four largest moons orbiting Jupiter were discovered by Galileo and are called the *Galilean moons.* One of them, Ganymede, is the biggest moon in our solar system. Ganymede is 5,276 kilometers

(3,278 miles) in diameter, even larger than the planet Mercury. Both Ganymede and Callisto, another of the Galilean moons, are bigger than Earth's moon. But the two other Galilean moons, Europa and Io, are about the same size as our moon.

If you could travel to Jupiter, you would not find it a very pleasant place. Jupiter's atmosphere is mainly hydrogen and helium, with some ammonia, methane, and water. You could not breathe this air. Thick clouds cover Jupiter. The temperature at the tops of the clouds is a very chilly -130° C (-210° F). As you approach Jupiter's surface, the temperature gets warmer. But the planet's surface is actually a vast ocean of liquid hydrogen. Astronomers believe the ocean is 20,000 kilometers (12,000 miles) deep.

A fascinating feature of Jupiter's atmosphere is the Great Red Spot near Jupiter's equator. Astronomers first noticed it 300 years ago. Today, astronomers think it is caused by an enormous hurricane. The spot moves slowly, but it has never gone away and shows no sign of disappearing.

See also **solar system** and **Galileo.**

The letter *K* began as an Egyptian word picture. It looked like a bowl or a cupped hand.

The Semites simplified the letter. They called it *kaph*, meaning "palm of the hand."

The ancient Greeks gave the letter the form it has today and passed it on to the Romans.

Kampuchea, *see* Cambodia

kangaroo

A kangaroo is easy to recognize. It has small front legs and often sits upright on large back legs, supporting itself with its large tail. It moves about by hopping or leaping on its powerful back legs, using its huge tail for balance. Kangaroos live only in Australia and on some nearby islands. In fact, the kangaroo is the national animal of Australia. There are about 55 kinds, including some called *wallabies*. The smallest is one kind of rat kangaroo that may be only 30 centimeters (1 foot) tall. The biggest are the gray and great red kangaroos, which may be taller than most adult humans.

The kangaroo can cover a lot of ground very quickly. A gray kangaroo—the kind most often seen in zoos—jumps over 1.8 meters (6 feet) of ground when it is just walking around. When it is in a hurry, each of its

Goodfellow's kangaroo (left) lives in trees. The red kangaroo (right) is a strong jumper.

leaps may be 9 meters (30 feet) long! As it jumps, the kangaroo holds its front legs close to its chest.

Except for the rat kangaroo, kangaroos are plant-eaters. Some need a lot of water. They live in swampy areas. Others can go without water for two months or longer. They live in desert areas. Kangaroos usually live in groups called *herds*. A herd of great red kangaroos may have more than 50 animals.

Most kangaroos live on the ground. But a few kinds live in trees. Unlike other kangaroos, tree kangaroos have front and back legs of equal size. Hooked claws on their back feet help them climb and hold onto branches.

Kangaroos are *marsupials*. This means the female has an outside pouch in which the newborn babies grow. A newborn kangaroo, called a *joey,* is only about 2.5 centimeters (1 inch) long. It climbs up its mother's body to her pouch, finding its way even though it cannot see. When it enters the pouch, it finds a nipple and starts to nurse. Over the next few months, the nursing joey gradually grows. Its eyes open, and it becomes covered with fur. When the joey is three or four months old, it begins to spend time outside its mother's pouch. Whenever it gets frightened or tired, it hops back into the pouch. Finally, when it is about six months old, it is too big to fit in the pouch. Even if the mother is pregnant, she will not give birth until the older joey has left her pouch. But once the older joey has left her pouch for good, the mother may have a new joey the very next day!

Kansas

Capital: Topeka
Area: 82,277 square miles (213,097 square kilometers) (14th-largest state)
Population (1980): 2,364,236 (1985): about 2,450,000 (32nd-largest state)
Became a state: January 29, 1861 (34th state)

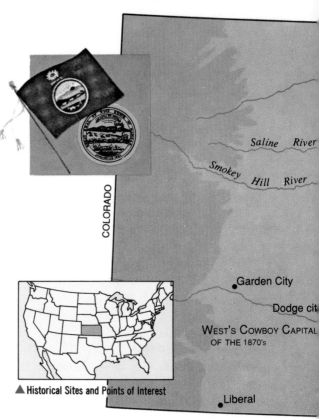

▲ Historical Sites and Points of Interest

If you put your finger right in the center of a map of the continental United States, you will be touching the state of Kansas. Kansas looks like a rectangle with a chunk missing in the northeastern corner.

Land Most of Kansas is flat or gently rolling. Kansas is a leading wheat-growing state, and it mills more flour than any other state. Kansas is also a leading cattle-raising state and has many meat-packing plants. It ranks high in the production of oil and natural gas.

Summers can be very hot and windy in Kansas. Winters are often very cold. Western Kansas gets only about 16 inches (41 centimeters) of rain a year, but eastern Kansas gets almost 42 inches (107 centimeters).

Kansas is in the "tornado belt." A *tornado* is a powerful storm. Its whirling winds do terrible damage wherever they touch the ground. Have you ever seen the movie *The Wizard of Oz*? Dorothy, the movie's main character, lives in Kansas, and her house is struck by a tornado. Many people in Kansas have a storm cellar or some other safe place to go during a tornado alert. (*See* **tornado**.)

History The Spanish explorer Francisco Vásquez de Coronado visited Kansas in 1541. He left because he did not find gold. Coronado and other Spaniards left a few horses behind. These were the first horses in the western United States. Within a hundred years, great herds of beautiful wild horses were roaming the Kansas plains.

In 1803, France sold the area that is now Kansas to the United States. This area was part of the Louisiana Purchase. (*See* **Louisiana Purchase**.)

In the 1820s, the U.S. government started to move tribes of Indians from the East onto land in Kansas. Traders began to cross Kansas at this time. In the 1840s, people went through Kansas on their way to California to look for gold.

In 1854, Kansas became a territory. Settlers from the South wanted slavery allowed. Northerners wanted it forbidden. There was so much fighting between these groups that the territory was called "Bleeding Kansas."

After the Civil War ended in 1865, many settlers, including freed slaves, came to Kansas. They were attracted by the Homestead Act. The Homestead Act gave 160 acres of land—free!—to anyone who would build a house, farm the land, and live on the land for five years.

At first, settlers in western Kansas had difficulty growing crops in the dry climate. But in 1874, a group of people called Mennonites arrived from a part of Russia that had a dry

28

NEBRASKA

Kirwin Reservoir

Republican River

Hanover

▲ ORIGINAL PONY EXPRESS STATION

Tuttle Creek Lake

Atchinson

Missouri River

FRONTIER OUTPOST AND HEADQUARTERS OF FIRST TERRITORIAL GOVERNOR

Kansas City

K A N S A S

Manhattan

Kansas River

Leavenworth

Topeka ★

Lawrence

Abilene

Junction City

HASKELL INSTITUTE INDIAN SCHOOL

Hays

Salina

BOYHOOD HOME OF D.D. EISENHOWER

Council Grove Lake

Ottawa

dar Bluff servoir

Kanopolis Lake

Emporia

Neosho River

Arkansas River

Great Bend

Fort Scott

Hutchinson

Newton

El Dorado

Chanute

Wichita

Pittsburg

Parsons

MISSOURI

HOME OF TEMPERANCE LEADER CARRY NATION

Medicine Lodge

Winfield

Independence

Arkansas City

Coffeyville

OKLAHOMA

Native sunflower

Western meadowlark

ELEVATION
Feet
3000 — 5000
2000 — 3000
1500 — 2000
1000 — 1500
600 — 1000

0   MILES   40

climate, too. They brought seeds for a kind of winter wheat that grew well in their dry homeland. Soon, many farmers in western Kansas were growing winter wheat.

The railroad towns of Abilene, Dodge City, and Wichita became famous as colorful "cow towns" in the 1870s. Cowboys drove huge herds of cattle from Texas to these towns. From there, the cattle were shipped by railroad to meat-packing plants in the East.

Wheat is the major crop in Kansas. Harvesters are at work at bottom.

In 1880, life in the cow towns became so wild that a law against alcoholic drinks was passed. Many towns paid no attention. A woman named Carry Nation decided to enforce it herself. She went into bars with a hatchet and smashed everything in sight. She tried to get laws passed against alcohol in the whole country. (*See* **Nation, Carry.**)

In the 1920s and 1930s, little rain fell in western Kansas. Terrible dust storms blew the soil away. Farmers lost their farms, and thousands of people moved to other states.

People Farming and ranching are still major activities in Kansas, but most Kansans live and work in cities. Wichita, the state's largest city, is the home of large aircraft factories. Kansas City, just across the river from Kansas City, Missouri, is the second-largest city. Kansas City, Kansas, is an important transportation center. It has many meat-packing plants and grain mills. Topeka, the capital, is the third-largest city.

Dwight D. Eisenhower, the 34th president of the United States, grew up in Kansas. His boyhood home and Presidential Library are in Abilene. (*See* **Eisenhower, Dwight D.**)

29

Helen Keller (left) "listens" to Anne Sullivan by touching her face as she talks.

Keller, Helen

Helen Keller was an American author and speaker admired throughout the world. From age two, she was deaf and blind. But she overcame her handicaps, and spent her life helping people with similar problems.

Keller was born in Tuscumbia, Alabama, in 1880. When she was 19 months old, a serious illness took away her sight and hearing. She could not learn to talk, because she could not hear other people talk. When she was angry, she kicked, scratched, and screamed. Finally, her parents wrote to the Perkins Institute for the Blind in Boston, Massachusetts, to ask for help. The institute sent a teacher for Helen. The teacher was Anne Sullivan.

Helen was almost seven years old when Anne Sullivan arrived. By spelling words out in the palm of Helen's hand, Sullivan taught the little girl that all things have names. *Water* was the first word Helen understood. She learned that words give people a way to communicate.

Sullivan went with Helen to schools in New York and Boston. Helen learned to read braille and to write on a special typewriter.

She learned to speak. With Anne Sullivan's help, she went to college. She graduated from Radcliffe College in 1904. (*See* **braille**.)

Keller's books and talks did much to make people aware of both the needs and abilities of handicapped people. She died in 1968.

kelp

Kelp is a kind of seaweed. It is a large alga that grows in cold, shallow oceans. It can be red, olive-green, or dark brown. It attaches itself to a rock or to the ocean floor. A long stem reaches to the surface. Giant grasslike or leaflike blades grow from the stem. Hollow balls, as small as marbles or as large as softballs, grow from the stem, too. These are filled with gas to help the kelp float near the surface. There it gets the sunlight it needs to grow. (*See* **algae**.)

In some places, kelp grows close together and forms large underwater forests. These give marine animals places to hide, live, and have their young. Some marine animals eat kelp. Others eat animals that live among the kelp. Sometimes, a kelp breaks loose and floats freely in the ocean. The floating kelp makes a giant mat where animals such as baby sea turtles can be safe.

Kelp is rich in iodine and potassium. It is used as a food, especially by the Japanese, and as a fertilizer for crops. Special ships harvest kelp. These ships move through kelp beds and chop off the tops of the plants. This does not harm the kelp, because it grows from the bottom.

Some kinds of kelp can grow to be nearly 100 feet (30 meters) long.

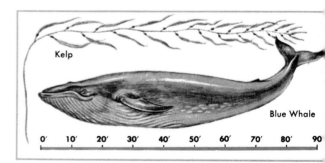

John F. Kennedy was the youngest person ever elected president.

Kennedy, John F.

John Fitzgerald Kennedy was the 35th president of the United States. He was the youngest man ever elected president—43 years old when he took office. People around the world admired his charm and his leadership. They were shocked and saddened when he was killed by a gunman less than three years after becoming president.

Kennedy was born in 1917 in Brookline, Massachusetts. After graduating from Harvard University, he joined the U.S. Navy. The United States was at war with Germany and Japan. Kennedy was put in charge of a PT boat—a small ship that carried weapons and was used for patrols. In 1943, the boat was destroyed by a Japanese ship in the Pacific Ocean. Two crew members died. Though Kennedy himself was injured, he led the rest of his men to safety. For this, he received the Navy and Marine Corps Medal and the Purple Heart.

After the war, Kennedy was elected a U.S. congressman from Boston. Then he was elected a U.S. senator from Massachusetts. In 1960, he became the Democratic party's candidate for president.

Kennedy ran against the Republican party's candidate, Richard Nixon. For the first time, two presidential candidates debated on television. Both answered questions and explained their opinions. John Kennedy's performance helped him win the election. He was the first Roman Catholic and the first Irish American to be elected president.

In his first speech as president, Kennedy said, "Ask not what your country can do for you—ask what you can do for your country." Kennedy thought public service was an important goal. He started the Peace Corps. Peace Corps members spend two years in poor countries, helping people improve their lives. Kennedy also supported laws to help blacks and other minorities receive equal treatment. (*See* **Peace Corps** and **civil rights.**)

Manned space flights became a reality in 1961, during the Kennedy presidency. Russia and the United States each tried for space "firsts." In 1962, John Glenn, Jr., became the first American to orbit Earth. (*See* **space exploration.**)

In 1962, the United States and Russia came to the brink of war over missile bases being built by Russia in communist Cuba. Kennedy blockaded Cuba with U.S. Navy ships and insisted that the bases be removed. After a very tense wait, Russia agreed, in exchange for a U.S. promise not to invade Cuba.

While in Dallas, Texas, in November 1963, Kennedy was *assassinated*—killed by a hidden attacker. Vice President Lyndon B. Johnson then became president. As president, Johnson worked to get Kennedy's proposals passed by Congress.

Kentucky

Capital: Frankfort
Area: 40,409 square miles (104,659 square kilometers) (37th-largest state)
Population (1980): 3,660,330 (1985): about 3,726,000 (23rd-largest state)
Became a state: June 1, 1792 (15th state)

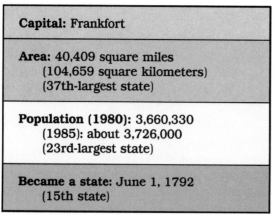

▲ Historical Sites and Points of Interest

Goldenrod

Cardinal

On a map, the state of Kentucky looks almost flat on the bottom, where it touches Tennessee. Its other sides twist and turn as they follow the rivers that form most of its boundaries.

Land Kentucky is in the south-central United States. Almost all of the state is hilly, and some of it is even mountainous. Kentucky has warm summers and mild winters. It receives about 46 inches (117 centimeters) of rain each year.

Much of the state's soil was formed from limestone. This fertile soil, combined with the mild climate, makes Kentucky an excellent place to grow crops or raise livestock. Kentucky's nickname is the "Bluegrass State," because of the blue-green grass that grows so well there.

Farming has been a major activity in Kentucky since the first European settlers arrived. Tobacco is an especially important crop. Only South Carolina grows more tobacco than Kentucky.

Western Kentucky is rich in coal. Coal has been mined in Kentucky since the 1870s, and the state still leads the nation in coal production.

Kentucky has several natural wonders. Mammoth Cave is the largest cave system in the world. Water has carved great caverns deep in the limestone. Some of the caverns are 200 feet (61 meters) high. So far, about 300 miles (483 kilometers) of underground

passageways have been explored. Echo River flows as deep as 360 feet (110 meters) beneath the surface.

Cumberland Falls is another of Kentucky's natural wonders. It is one of only two waterfalls in the world that has a "moonbow." A moonbow is formed when moonlight is reflected on spray from a waterfall.

Big Bone Lick is a natural salt spring. Bones of mammoths and mastodons have been found at Big Bone. So scientists know that even prehistoric animals came there to lick the salt.

History People, too, have lived in Kentucky since prehistoric times. Ancient Indians called Mound Builders lived there. They piled up earth into small hills, where they buried their dead.

Beginning in 1669, French and English people explored eastern and southern Kentucky. They did not find any Indians living there. But Indian tribes to the north and south fought many bloody wars with each other over the right to use the area as a hunting ground.

Few settlers came to Kentucky before 1750. It was too difficult to bring wagons over the rugged Appalachian Mountains in

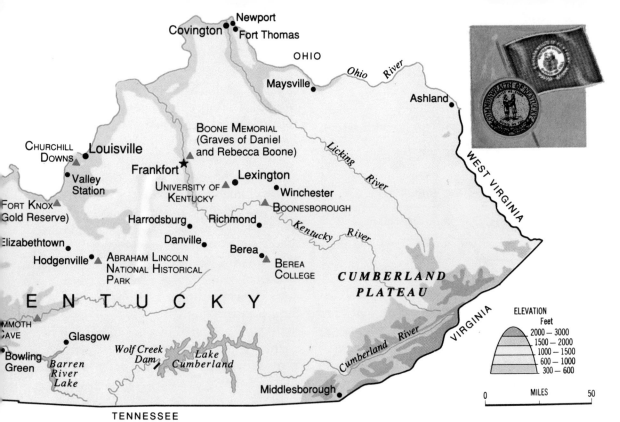

Newport
Covington
Fort Thomas

OHIO

Maysville

Ohio River

Ashland

Boone Memorial
(Graves of Daniel
and Rebecca Boone)

Churchill
Downs
Louisville

Frankfort

University of
Kentucky
Lexington
Winchester
Boonesborough

Licking River

WEST VIRGINIA

Valley
Station

Fort Knox
Gold Reserve)

Harrodsburg
Richmond

Kentucky River

Elizabethtown

Hodgenville
Abraham Lincoln
National Historical
Park
Danville
Berea
Berea
College

K E N T U C K Y

CUMBERLAND
PLATEAU

MMOTH
AVE

Glasgow

Wolf Creek
Dam
Lake
Cumberland

VIRGINIA

Cumberland River

Bowling
Green
Barren
River
Lake

Middlesborough

TENNESSEE

ELEVATION
Feet
2000 – 3000
1500 – 2000
1000 – 1500
600 – 1000
300 – 600

0   MILES   50

the east. But in 1750, a passage through the mountains was discovered. People named it the Cumberland Gap. (*See* **Cumberland Gap.**)

Daniel Boone was one of the first white men to explore central and northern Kentucky. He led settlers through the Cumberland Gap and showed them good places to build villages. (*See* **Boone, Daniel.**)

Kentucky was the first area west of the Appalachian Mountains to be settled by American pioneers. Most of the pioneers came

Kentucky is famous for the racehorses and show horses that are trained there.

from Virginia or North Carolina. At first, Kentucky was part of Virginia. It became a separate state in 1792.

Kentucky's leaders tried to keep the state out of the Civil War, but many battles were fought in Kentucky. Kentucky allowed slavery, but it did not leave the Union. Some Kentuckians fought for the North and some fought for the South.

People More Kentuckians live on farms or in small towns than in big cities. There are two large cities. The largest is Louisville, an important manufacturing and trade center. It is also the home of the Kentucky Derby, the most famous horse race in the United States. The derby has been held every year since 1785. Now it is held on the first Saturday in May.

Kentucky's second-largest city is Lexington. It is in the beautiful Bluegrass region. This area is known for the thoroughbred racehorses raised there.

Kentucky has many "famous sons." Abraham Lincoln, the 16th president of the United States, was born near Hodgenville and lived in the state until he was seven. Jefferson Davis, president of the Confederate States of America, was born in Kentucky.

Kenya

Capital: Nairobi
Area: 224,960 square miles (582,646 square kilometers)
Population (1985): about 20,194,000
Official language: Swahili

Kenya is a country in eastern Africa. It is about as big as the state of Texas and is a land of great variety. There are mountains and plains, rich farmland, and dry desert. Kenya has a seacoast on the Indian Ocean.

People from many African tribes live in Kenya. They have their own languages, customs, and religions. One group, the Masai, are *nomads*—herders who wander in search of food. (*See* **nomad.**)

Kenya is also known for its huge wildlife *refuges.* In the refuges, lions, elephants, giraffes, leopards, zebras, and many other animals live safely in the wild.

The equator runs through the center of Kenya, giving much of the country a very warm climate all year. But the southern part of Kenya has high mountains and a mild climate. Mount Kenya, Africa's second-tallest mountain, is near the equator but is always capped with snow. Kenya's main export crops, coffee and tea, grow well in the mountains. Kenya's capital and largest city, Nairobi, is in the south.

Much of central Kenya is a high plain covered by grass and patches of forest. Great herds of wild animals live here. It is a popular place for *safaris*—trips into the country to see the wildlife. Kenya's northern regions are mostly dry desert.

For thousands of years, the lands of Kenya were used by many different African tribes. After A.D. 700, Muslim traders visited from the north. They took some people captive and sold them as slaves.

In the 1800s, Europeans reached Kenya. Missionaries from Europe and the United States came to teach Christianity. Later, in 1890, Great Britain made Kenya a colony.

In the 1950s, Kenyans began to demand independence. They rebelled against British

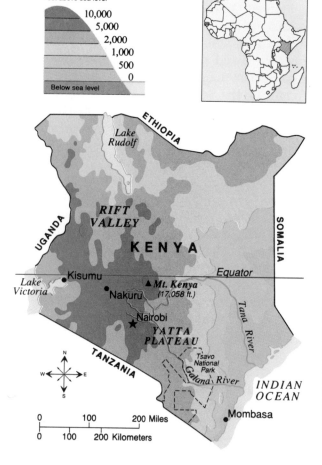

Elephants stop for a drink at a game refuge in Kenya's grasslands.

rule and fought many bloody battles against the British. Finally, in 1963, Kenya gained its independence.

Jomo Kenyatta was Kenya's first president. In 15 years as president, he became one of Africa's most respected leaders. He helped his country grow peacefully.

When Kenyatta died, in 1978, many groups tried to gain control of the government. Still, Kenya remains one of the more prosperous African nations.

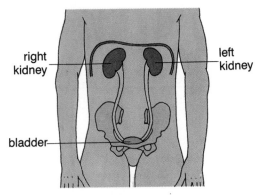

The kidneys, in the upper abdomen behind the liver and stomach, are connected to the bladder at the bottom of the abdomen.

kidney

Your body cells are constantly producing waste products. Your blood picks up these wastes and carries some of them to the kidneys. There, the wastes are removed from the blood and leave the body as urine.

If the wastes are not removed, they build up in the blood and become poisonous. Fortunately, you have two kidneys. There is one on each side of your spine, above the small of the back and below the rib cage. Each kidney is shaped like a bean and is about the size of your fist. If one kidney fails, the other can handle the job by itself.

Almost 200 liters (50 gallons) of blood pass through the kidneys each day. Inside the kidneys are tiny coiled tubes, each with a little cup called a *capsule* at the end. When blood enters the kidneys, it goes to the capsules, where the waste products are removed. Then the waste products flow through the tiny coiled tubes. They collect in the center of the kidneys, in the form of urine. The urine goes to the bladder, where it is stored until it leaves the body. The clean blood leaves the kidneys and returns to the circulatory system. (*See* **blood circulation.**)

King, Billie Jean

Billie Jean King was a great U.S. tennis star of the 1960s and 1970s. In the U.S. Open tournament, she won the women's singles title four times. She won 20 titles in singles and doubles play at Wimbledon, the British tournament. This set a record that no male or female tennis player has ever broken.

Billie Jean Moffitt was born in California in 1943. She married Larry King in 1965. She believed that tournaments should award women and men the same amount of prize money. In 1971, King became the first woman athlete in any sport to earn more than $100,000 in one year. A year later, *Sports Illustrated* magazine named her "Sportsman of the Year."

In 1973, the prize money for men and women at the U.S. Open was made equal. That same year, in a famous match, King defeated Bobby Riggs,

See also **tennis.**

Billie Jean King waits to return a shot.

King, Martin Luther, Jr.

Martin Luther King, Jr., led a movement during the 1950s and 1960s to bring about equal rights for black Americans. King and his followers did not use violence. Their work helped bring into law the Civil Rights Act of 1964 and the Voting Rights Act of 1965. These laws were a step in ending the unfair treatment of American citizens because of their race.

King was born in Atlanta, Georgia, in 1929. His father was the pastor of the Ebenezer Baptist Church, and his mother was the church's choir director. King studied for the ministry and earned a degree from Boston University. He met and later married a fellow student, Coretta Scott. King became pastor of the Dexter Avenue Baptist Church in Montgomery, Alabama, in 1954.

As pastor, King became active in the fight to end the unjust treatment of people because of race. In Montgomery, as in other places across the nation, blacks were *segregated*—kept apart—from whites, often by law. Blacks, for example, had to ride in the back of public buses, while whites could ride in front.

In 1955, King urged Montgomery's blacks not to ride the buses as a protest. This action was called a *boycott.* Over the next year, the bus boycott led to many physical attacks on blacks. But King urged his followers not to strike back with violence. "We will not degrade ourselves with hatred," he said. "Love will be returned for hate." The boycott cost the bus company a lot of money. In the end, the company agreed to end segregation on its buses. Soon, segregation laws were being changed all over the South.

During the following years, King made many speeches. He wanted laws that would protect the *civil rights* of all races. Civil rights are the freedoms, such as freedom of speech and freedom to gather in groups, promised to all Americans by the Constitution. In 1963, 250,000 Americans marched in Washington, D.C., to show Congress that

Martin Luther King speaks during a civil rights campaign in 1966.

©1966 Flip Schulke

they supported equal rights. At the march, King gave one of the most famous speeches in U.S. history. He told the crowd, "I have a dream that my four little children will one day live in a nation where they will not be judged by the color of their skin, but by the content of their character."

People across the world were moved by King's speech and by his work. King was awarded the Nobel Peace Prize in 1964. He was killed by a gunman in Memphis, Tennessee, in 1968.

See also **civil rights.**

kings and queens

Kings and queens are *monarchs*—people who rule whole countries—*kingdoms*—without being elected. Instead, their power is handed down by parents who ruled before them. They usually rule for life. Sometimes, however, a person becomes king or queen by taking power by force. (*See* **monarchy.**)

When it is the king who inherits power, his wife is made queen. If it is the queen who inherits the throne, her husband is given a royal title but is not usually made king. In the past, kings and queens held complete power over their *subjects*—the people who lived in their kingdoms. Kings and queens could settle arguments among their subjects, or decide whether someone was guilty of a crime. Even if kings and queens did not fight on the battlefield, they were the leaders of their kingdoms' military. It was the duty of the subjects to obey the king and queen. In return, the king and queen were to rule wisely and fairly.

A few countries still have a king or queen at the head of the government. Denmark, Sweden, Great Britain, the Netherlands, and Belgium have a king or queen, or both. Morroco, in Africa, is ruled by a king. Today's kings and queens usually have little power. But people still respect their king and queen. Even if other leaders in a country change, the king and queen are always there. In Great Britain, after a movie, the audience sings "God Save the Queen."

In the past, many nations were ruled by kings and queens. Old African nations and the ancient Israelites were ruled by kings. Ancient Egypt was ruled by kings, called *pharaohs,* and queens. In the country of Turkey, the kings were called *sultans.* A king who ruled a very large kingdom, such as China, was called an *emperor,* and the queen was called an *empress.* (*See* **Africa; Israelites;** and **Egypt, ancient.**)

Some of the most famous kings and queens ruled in Europe, beginning about the year 1000. Many European monarchs were famous military leaders. A French lord defeated the English in 1066 and became their king. He is known as William the Conqueror. Another military king of England was Richard the Lion-Hearted, one of William's descendants. He spent very little time ruling England because he was busy fighting a religious war. (*See* **Crusades.**)

Kiribati, *see* Pacific Islands

At left, Charlemagne, king of the Franks, becomes Holy Roman Emperor in the year 800. At right, Beatrix at her coronation as queen of the Netherlands in 1980.

poleax

basinet

ventail

jupon

hauberk

foot soldier
with chain mail
(1100s)

Normandy 1000

France 1500

Knights wore heavy armor
for protection. Often, knights fought
on horseback (above right).

knighthood

Hundreds of years ago, Europe was divided into many small areas ruled by kings and by nobles called *lords*. Powerful lords had their own armies of mounted soldiers called *knights*. At first, a boy became a knight simply by going to fight for his lord. Later, people worked out a detailed set of rules about knighthood. These were widely followed, especially in France, Spain, and England, from about 1100 to 1300.

To become a knight, a boy went through years of training. First, around age seven, he became a *page*. As a page, he lived in the lord's household and served the family. He learned to ride a horse and fight with a small sword. A page became a *squire* around age 15. As a squire, he continued his training, but now with real weapons. A squire also served a knight. He stood by the knight at meals and fought beside him.

By the time he was 20, the squire was ready to become a knight. The ceremony included a night of prayer alone in church.

The next day, the young man knelt before his lord. The lord tapped his shoulder with a sword and said, "I dub you knight."

Knights wore metal suits called *armor* for protection in battle. Metal helmets covered their heads and faces. Metal gloves called *gauntlets* covered their hands. When knights were not fighting, they held contests called *tournaments.* In these, they practiced their fighting skills. Two knights on horseback, carrying lances, might line up on opposite sides of the field and charge each other. Each knight tried to knock his opponent off his horse. This was called a *joust.* Although most knights used weapons with dull points in these contests, many were injured and some were even killed.

Knights were supposed to follow a code of behavior known as *chivalry.* The rules of chivalry required a knight to be a good Christian, loyal to his lord, and fearless in battle. Chivalry also required courtesy toward women. In fact, the idea of romantic love—tender devotion between a man and a woman—began with chivalry.

Knighthood and chivalry inspired many songs, poems, and legends. The most famous were the stories about King Arthur and his Knights of the Round Table. (*See* **Arthur, King.**)

Today, in England, knighthood still exists as an honor. The king or queen grants knighthood to men and women who have done important things for society. A man who becomes a knight is addressed as "Sir." A woman who is knighted is known as "Dame."

See also **Middle Ages.**

knitting and crocheting

Knitting and crocheting (cro-SHAY-ing) are ways to make cloth and clothing by looping yarn over special needles. You can easily make beautiful designs by either knitting or crocheting.

Knitting may be done on one circular needle or on two or more straight needles. The kind and size you use depend on what you are knitting. You can knit scarves, socks, sweaters, mittens, and other things.

Knitting has two basic stitches—*knit* and *purl.* Many fancy designs can be made either by using knit or purl stitches alone, or by using the two together. Other designs are made by changing the color of the yarn as you go.

Crocheting uses one needle. One end is hooked to catch hold of a strand of yarn and pull a loop of it through other loops of yarn. The basic stitches are the *chain stitch, single crochet,* and *double crochet.*

Knitting and crocheting are very old crafts. In France, China, Italy, and Ireland, crocheting has long been used to make beautiful lace. People all over the world still enjoy knitting and crocheting by hand. But today, machines make most lace and do most of the knitting.

knots

Knots are fastenings made by tying pieces of rope, cord, string, or fabric. Some knots are used for tying pieces of rope together. Some knots tie one thing to another.

There are three basic kinds of knots—*knots, hitches,* and *bends.* In a knot, a cord is pulled through a loop. Knots are used for tying bundles and making nooses and loops. Hitches are used to fasten a rope to an object, such as a post. Bends are used to tie two ropes together.

Knots have hundreds of uses. Sailors need to use them often. People who go camping tie knots to fasten tent lines and hold other objects. Horseback riders use knots to hitch their horses so the horses cannot run away.

TYPES OF KNOTS

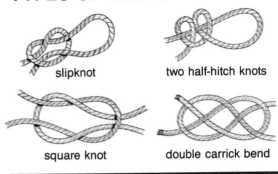

slipknot

two half-hitch knots

square knot

double carrick bend

Farmers have many uses for knots around their farms.

There are also more unusual uses for knots. The ancient Incas of South America used knotted ropes called *quipus* to keep count of supplies and people. Fishermen use knots to make their nets. The handcraft of macramé is an arrangement of knots. Some people make interesting knots to use as buttons. (*See* **Inca.**)

koala

The koala (ko-AH-la) looks like a gray teddy bear with hairy ears. But koalas are not bears. Koalas live in eucalyptus forests in Australia. They eat only the leaves and buds of certain eucalyptus trees. They need about a kilogram (2 pounds) of leaves each day. If they cannot find enough of these trees, they starve to death. They do not drink water at

A koala feasts on eucalyptus leaves, its only food.

all. Instead, they get their water from the leaves. The name *koala* means "no drink."

An adult koala is about 60 centimeters (2 feet) long and weighs up to 14 kilograms (31 pounds). It has short, strong legs and strong claws on its feet. It uses the claws to climb trees. Koalas spend most of their time in trees. They sleep on high branches during the day. At night, they travel from tree to tree in search of food.

Koalas are *marsupials*. This means the females have a pouch in which the babies are raised. A baby koala is very tiny at birth—less than 2 centimeters (1 inch) long! But it is strong enough to crawl into its mother's pouch, where it stays until it is about six months old. When it comes out, the baby koala clings to its mother's fur. Sometimes, it rides on her back. Once it is about a year old, it begins to travel on its own.

Koran

The Koran is the sacred book of Islam, one of the world's major religions. Muslims are followers of Islam. They believe the Koran is the word of Allah. *Allah* is the Arabic name for God. It is the duty of every Muslim to study the Koran.

Islam was started by Muhammad, an Arab prophet, in the 600s. According to Islamic belief, Allah spoke to Muhammad through Gabriel, an angel. Muhammad then told people what Gabriel said, and his followers wrote down the words. These teachings were collected to form the Koran.

The Koran is written in rhymes and in the Arabic language. It contains 114 chapters, called *suras*. Some chapters tell stories about the prophets Allah sent to teach his people. These prophets include Abraham, Moses, and Jesus Christ. According to the Koran, Muhammad is Allah's last prophet.

The Koran also tells Muslims how they should live and worship. It says that one day people will have to appear before Allah and account for the way they have lived. Prayers from the Koran are recited during Islamic services on Friday afternoons.

See also **Islam.**

Korea

South Korea
Capital: Seoul
Area: 38,025 square miles (98,485 square kilometers)
Population (1985): about 42,643,000
Official language: Korean

North Korea
Capital: Pyongyang
Area: 46,540 square miles (120,539 square kilometers)
Population (1985): about 20,082,000
Official language: Korean

Korea is a land in eastern Asia. Since the 1950s, it has been divided into two nations, North Korea and South Korea. Korea is a peninsula—it is surrounded on three sides by water. To the west is the Yellow Sea. To the east and the south is the sea of Japan. On the north, Korea borders China and the Soviet Union.

Korea has rugged mountains, but the fertile valleys are good for growing huge crops of rice. Korean farms also produce wheat, barley, beans, potatoes, corn, and millet.

North Korea has more land than South Korea. But South Korea has more than twice as many people. South Korea's capital, Seoul, is one of the five largest cities in the world.

Korea has been strongly influenced by China. Most Koreans have the same ancestors as the Chinese. Their languages and

Above, South Korean art students sketch an ancient palace in Seoul. Below, workers on an automobile assembly line in South Korea. Korean manufactured goods are sold in many parts of the world.

writing are similar. Two religions widely followed in Korea—Buddhism and Confucianism—also came from China. Buddhism is Korea's most important religion. But many South Koreans are Christians.

For centuries, Korea ruled itself. But in the late 1800s, it became a battleground for three powerful neighbors—China, Russia, and Japan. Japan controlled Korea from 1910 to 1945. Then Japan was defeated in World War II. (*See* **World War II.**)

Two nations that were allies in World War II—the United States and the Soviet Union—wanted Korea to be independent. But each wanted the new country as a friend, so they divided it in two. North Korea became a close friend of the Soviet Union and China. South Korea became a close friend of the United States.

41

North and South Korea became bitter enemies. In 1950, communist North Koreans invaded the South, hoping to make one Korea again. The United Nations sent soldiers to help South Korea. The Korean War went on for three years, but neither side won. Finally, they agreed to stop fighting and to remain divided. (*See* **Korean War.**)

Since then, both North and South Korea have become important industrial nations. North Korea produces iron and steel, and both countries produce textiles, chemicals, machinery, and processed foods.

Korean War

The Korean War was fought from 1950 until 1953 in Korea, a country that juts out from the Asian mainland, east of China. The fighting involved armies from many countries, including the United States and the Soviet Union. The war also tested the strength of the newly formed United Nations.

American soldiers march to the battlefield as Korean women and children hurry away.

Throughout its history, Korea has been influenced by two powerful neighbors—China and Japan. Japan ruled Korea from 1910 until the end of World War II, in 1945. After that war, armed forces from the Soviet Union occupied the northern half of Korea, and troops from the United States were sent to the southern part. An imaginary line, called the *38th parallel,* divided North Korea from South Korea.

The United Nations (U.N.) had been founded to protect world peace. The U.N. decided that an election should be held to set up one national government in Korea. The Soviet Union did not like the idea. In 1948, two separate governments were established instead. South Korea elected members to an assembly and created the Republic of Korea. The North Korean Communists set up the Democratic People's Republic of Korea. Both governments claimed to rule all of Korea.

On June 25, 1950, troops from North Korea invaded South Korea. South Korea asked the U.N. for help. The U.N. asked its member nations to send troops and supplies to South Korea. The American general Douglas MacArthur was put in charge of the U.N. forces. He was later replaced by Lieutenant General Matthew B. Ridgway. Soldiers from 16 U.N. countries went to South Korea. Weapons and food supplies came from 41 U.N. countries. But more than half of the troops and weapons sent to South Korea came from the United States. Chinese soldiers fought on the side of the North Koreans, and the Soviet Union gave them weapons.

The fighting was long and bloody. Over 2 million soldiers were killed, wounded, or reported lost. About a million South Korean citizens were killed, too. Peace talks began in 1951, but an agreement was not reached until 1953. In the end, Korea remained divided into two countries.

See also **Korea; United Nations;** and **MacArthur, Douglas.**

Kuwait, *see* Middle East

The letter *L* was once an Egyptian word picture. It was the symbol for a kind of stick called a *goad*.

When the Semites borrowed the symbol, they turned it around and called it *lamed*, their word for "goad."

The Greeks added it to their alphabet and called it *lambda*. They wrote it as an upside-down *V*.

Labor Day

Labor Day is a holiday in honor of people who work. In the United States and Canada, Labor Day is celebrated on the first Monday in September. It is a *legal holiday,* which means that most businesses and government offices are closed.

Matthew Maguire, of New Jersey, and Peter J. McGuire, a leader of a New York carpenters' union, are thought to have first suggested a day for honoring workers. The first Labor Day parade was held in New York City in 1882. At that time, it was not yet a holiday. Oregon was the first state to make Labor Day a holiday. In 1894, it became an official national holiday in the United States.

Parades are an important part of Labor Day. So are speeches by labor leaders. Some people have picnics or just relax. For many, Labor Day marks the end of summer. Soon after Labor Day, many schools begin their new year.

In most of Europe, Labor Day is celebrated on May 1. In the Soviet Union and other communist countries, May 1 is May Day, an important holiday.

labor union

A labor union is a group of workers who have joined together to make agreements with the companies they work for. A single worker may have a hard time getting higher pay or safer working conditions. But together in a union, workers have more bargaining power.

In the 1800s, workers in factories had no power. If they wanted to keep their jobs, they had to work as long as the factory owners wanted, for whatever the factory owners wanted to pay. Many people worked from 7:00 in the morning to 7:00 at night, six days a week. Workers were paid too little to support a family. So children began working in factories as early as age seven.

Workers formed the first unions to get better working conditions. Factory owners often threatened to fire all workers who belonged to a union. Unions sometimes called *strikes* —stopped work—to force owners to give in. Little by little, unions succeeded in gaining better conditions and higher pay.

Striking workers form a picket line. Other union members usually will not cross the line to go to work.

Today, many workers belong to unions. Union representatives meet with the company's managers to *negotiate*—work out an agreement. They negotiate how much union members should be paid for their work, what hours they should work, and other matters. If the union representatives and the managers cannot agree, the union may call a strike. During a strike, union members do not work, and they are not paid by the company. Their union may give them *strike pay* while union leaders and company managers try to reach an agreement.

Labrador, *see* Newfoundland

Lafayette, Marquis de

The Marquis de Lafayette (mar-KEY duh la-fay-ET) was a French nobleman. He helped the American colonists during the Revolutionary War against Great Britain. His military skills made him a hero.

Lafayette was born in 1757 into a wealthy family. His name was Marie Joseph Paul Yves Roch Gilbert de Motier. When his grandfather died, the boy inherited the title Marquis de Lafayette.

As a boy, Lafayette began studying to be a soldier. In 1777, when he was 19, he became excited by the American colonies' fight for independence. He decided to go to America and help fight against Great Britain, which was an enemy of France. The Americans were pleased to have such a well-trained young soldier. They made him a major general, and he went immediately into battle. He became a friend of the colonies' commander, George Washington. For four years, he helped the colonial troops. In 1781, he commanded one of the armies that surrounded the British and made them surrender.

Lafayette returned home to France and became a leader in the French Revolution, which began in 1789.

See also **Revolutionary War; Valley Forge;** and **French Revolution.**

lake

A lake is a body of water surrounded by land. Some lakes are so large that you cannot see across them. Others are only a few hundred feet across. Small lakes are sometimes called *ponds.*

Lakes fill bowl-shaped areas in the ground, called *basins.* Lake basins form in many different ways. Some are the craters of ancient volcanoes. Many lake basins were made by *glaciers*—huge sheets of ice that scraped across the land.

Lakes can also be made by beavers or people. When beavers dam a stream, the water backs up and forms a pond. People have built dams across great rivers and made lakes more than 100 miles (160 kilometers) long. Lake Powell, in Arizona and Utah, is a lake of this kind. (*See* **dam.**)

Most lakes and ponds contain fresh water, not salt water. The water is passing through these lakes on its way to an ocean. The water travels through streams and rivers from the lake to the ocean.

The Great Lakes in North America are huge freshwater lakes. One of them, Lake Superior, is the biggest freshwater lake in the world. Water flows eastward from one Great Lake to another. Then the water flows to the Atlantic Ocean through the St. Lawrence River. (*See* **Great Lakes.**)

The region around the Great Lakes has thousands of small lakes and ponds. In fact, the state of Minnesota is called the "Land of 10,000 Lakes."

A few lakes have no outlet to the sea. These lakes have salty water. Water can leave this kind of lake only through evaporation. But many chemicals dissolved in the water do not evaporate. They are left behind

There are lakes at many different elevations. Water runs downhill from freshwater lakes into the oceans.

Dead Sea

Caspian Sea

In part of northern Canada, lakes stretch as far as the eye can see.

WORLD'S LARGEST LAKES

Name	Location	Area Square Miles	Area Square Kilometers
Caspian Sea	Soviet Union, Iran	143,630	372,000
Lake Superior	U.S., Canada	31,700	82,103
Lake Victoria	Africa	26,828	69,484
Aral Sea	Soviet Union	25,660	66,459
Lake Huron	U.S., Canada	23,050	59,699
Lake Michigan	U.S.	22,300	57,757
Lake Tanganyika	Africa	12,700	32,893
Great Bear Lake	Canada	12,275	31,792
Lake Baikal	Soviet Union	12,162	31,499
Lake Nyasa	Africa	11,100	28,749
Great Slave Lake	Canada	10,980	28,438
Lake Erie	U.S., Canada	9,889	25,612
Lake Winnipeg	Canada	9,465	24,514
Lake Ontario	U.S., Canada	7,313	18,941
Lake Ladoga	Soviet Union	7,100	18,389
Lake Chad	Africa	7,000	18,130
Lake Balkhash	Soviet Union	6,680	17,300
Lake Maracaibo	Venezuela	5,200	13,500
Lake Onega	Soviet Union	3,800	9,892

in the lake and make the water salty. Because a salty lake has no outlet, it grows or shrinks from one year to the next. If there is a lot of rain and snow, the lake fills up and covers a larger area. During dry years, it gets smaller.

The Caspian Sea, between the Soviet Union and Iran, is actually a salty lake. In fact, it is the world's largest lake. Other salty lakes include Great Salt Lake in Utah and the Dead Sea between Israel and Jordan. The Dead Sea is almost 400 meters (1,300 feet) below sea level. It is the lowest body of water on earth. (*See* **Caspian Sea; Great Salt Lake;** and **Dead Sea.**)

between six weeks and three months old. If the sheep is over a year old, the meat is called *mutton.*

Lamb is not a favorite meat in most of the United States. Most Americans prefer to eat beef. But people in many parts of North Africa and the Middle East prefer lamb to other meats. Lamb is also a favorite in Australia, New Zealand, England, and Greece.

Lamb chops and leg of lamb are the most popular lamb dishes in the United States. Lamb chops are usually broiled or fried. Leg of lamb is often roasted with the bone still inside. Some people serve a roasted rack of lamb, which includes the ribs. Many enjoy lamb shanks, which come from the front

lamb

The meat from any sheep under one year old is called lamb. Most of the lamb eaten in the United States comes from animals that are

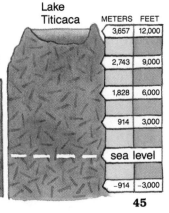

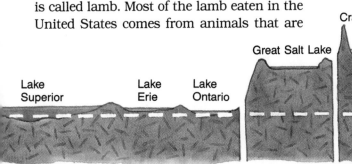

legs and shoulder. Lamb is also good in stews.

During the Jewish holy day of Passover, a special meal, called a *seder,* includes roast lamb. In Greece and some other Christian countries, lamb is part of the traditional Easter feast. (*See* **Passover** and **Easter.**)

landslide

A landslide is a large amount of rock and soil that falls from the side of a mountain or the wall of a canyon. Some people call such falls *avalanches,* but an avalanche is a fall of snow and ice. (*See* **avalanche.**)

Some landslides are caused by earthquakes. In 1959, an earthquake in western Montana caused a large landslide. This landslide blocked a canyon and killed more than a dozen campers.

Other landslides happen when heavy rain or melting snow seeps into a hillside. The water loosens the soil and rock. In 1903, in Alberta, Canada, a large landslide that began this way buried most of a small town and killed 70 people.

A mudflow is a special kind of landslide. It is so full of water that it flows instead of falling. A volcano that erupted in 1985 in Colombia, South America, caused a mudflow. The volcano's heat melted ice and snow on its sides very quickly. The mudflow came rushing down, killing more than 10,000 people.

language

Language is the way that people communicate with each other by speaking or writing. Other animals communicate, too, but their ways of communicating are not usually called languages.

There are now about 3,000 different languages spoken in the world. Some are spoken by millions of people. Others are spoken by just a few hundred. Many old languages have disappeared.

Anyone who travels to other countries knows that people speak different languages. The languages use different words and put them together in different ways. Each language also has its own sounds. For

After heavy rains, a part of a hillside in Southern California slid away. The landslide destroyed a house perched on top of the hill and partly buried it.

Language may have started as an imitation of sounds in nature.

example, some languages spoken in Africa use click sounds. In English, we may use clicks to make noises for babies or animals, but they are not part of our language.

People who study languages are called *linguists*. Many linguists believe that humans have always used languages. For thousands of years, people spoke but did not have writing. Today, we have no way of knowing what those spoken languages were like. Around 3500 B.C., people began to write. Linguists study written languages to learn how languages have changed over time.

History of Languages One of the great mysteries in the world is how languages began. Nobody knows. Many linguists think people began speaking by imitating sounds. Animals make some noises that have certain meanings. Humans may have begun to speak in the same way—by making noises. Even if that is true, we do not know how people began to turn the noises into words and put the words into sentences.

Another great mystery about languages is whether all languages came from one parent language. Or did different language families begin in different places? If all of today's languages came from one parent language, perhaps someday linguists will figure out how all languages are related.

Language Families This book is written in the English language. English is one of many languages in a family of languages called *Indo-European*. Linguists believe that all the languages in the Indo-European family came from one ancient language. They have found many connections among the languages in this family.

Almost half of the world's people speak a language in the Indo-European family. The family includes the ancient language Sanskrit, which was once spoken in India. It includes the ancient languages spoken in Egypt, Greece, and Rome. It also includes the languages spoken today in nearly every country of Europe, the Middle East, and North Africa. Some of these languages are now spoken by most people in North and South America and Australia as well.

The ancient Romans spoke Latin, which is not spoken anymore. But many present-day languages grew out of Latin—French, Italian, Portuguese, Romanian, and Spanish.

English is part of the Germanic group of Indo-European languages. Its closest relatives are German, Dutch, Danish, and Swedish. English also has many words from Latin. (*See* **English language.**)

The languages of China and China's neighbors belong to another large family of languages, called *Sino-Tibetan.* Mandarin Chinese is one of the many languages in this

Most European languages are related to each other, so some common words are much alike. The languages may all have come from a single ancestor language.

English	mother	father	brother	sister
Old English	mōdor	faeder	brōthor	sweoster
German	Mutter	Vater	Bruder	Schwester
Latin	mater	pater	frater	soror
Italian	madre	padre	fratello	sorella
Spanish	madre	padre	hermano	hermana
French	mère	père	frère	soeur

Left, English changed an Indian word so that it sounded like two English words.
Right, British English and American English often have different words for the same thing.

family. More people speak Mandarin Chinese than any other language in the world. Many Sino-Tibetan languages are *tonal.* This means that when people speak, the pitch of their voice—high or low, going up or going down—is part of the word. The same syllable may have different meanings when spoken in different tones.

Changes in Languages Linguists know that all languages change as time passes. Old words gain new meanings. New words come into the languages because people have new ideas and inventions. People borrow words from other languages.

English, for example, has borrowed words from many languages. The word *kindergarten* comes from German; *pizza* from Italian, *raccoon* from an American Indian language, *bungalow* from a language spoken in India, and *coffee* from Arabic. Other languages borrow words from English, too.

Languages also change from place to place. The English spoken in England or Australia can be understood by Americans who speak English, but some words are different. Americans say *elevator;* the English say *lift.* Americans say *cookie;* the English say *biscuit.* People in English-speaking countries may also pronounce many words differently.

Linguists believe that the spoken, not the written, language is the true language. People are always thinking of new ways to say

things, and bringing new words and phrases into the language. For example, new inventions and space exploration have brought new words into the language. Among these are *printout, videodisk, laser,* and *splashdown.*

Written language changes more slowly. Linguists believe that writing is only a way of keeping track of the spoken language. It is a record of how people have talked.

Learning Languages The language a person learns first is called his or her *native language.* Many people learn a second, third, and even a fourth language. Sometimes they learn it because they live in a country that uses more than one language. Canada, for example, has two main languages—English and French.

Other people learn new languages because they need them for business or education. In many parts of the world, people learn English as a second language.

Invented Languages Some languages are not really the native language of any group of people. Many languages, called *pidgin,* are made up from words of different languages. In some Pacific Islands, the people speak their own language to each other. But to outsiders, they speak Pidgin English. It has many English words, but also many words from other languages. Pidgin languages were first used among traders who spoke different languages.

Esperanto is an invented language taking words from several European languages.

The best-known invented language is *Esperanto.* The people who invented it hoped that all the people in the world would learn it. They believed that if people spoke the same language, they would understand each other better and get along more peacefully.

Laos, *see* Asia

Lapland, *see* Scandinavia

larva

A caterpillar is the larva of a butterfly or a moth. A tadpole is the larva of a frog. Many insects and some other animals change their forms as they develop. This kind of development is called *metamorphosis.* In metamorphosis, the creature goes through separate stages. It is an egg, then a larva, then an adult. When the creature is a larva, it is still immature. It must develop further before it becomes an adult and can reproduce.

A larva turns into an adult quite different from itself. Tadpoles become frogs, and caterpillars become butterflies or moths.

billbug larva

tadpole

buckeye butterfly caterpillar

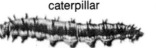

Besides changing its shape, many parts inside the larva's body change, too. For example, a tadpole breathes by means of gills. An adult frog breathes by means of lungs. During metamorphosis, the tadpole loses its gills and develops lungs.

Larvae (the plural of *larva*) often live in a way that is different from the way their parents live. For example, starfish larvae swim. They live near the surface of the sea, where they eat tiny plants. When the larvae have grown, they sink to the bottom of the sea. There they change into adult starfish. The adults move by crawling. They eat clams and other animals.

See also **life cycle; caterpillar; amphibian;** and **insect.**

La Salle, Sieur de

La Salle was a French explorer. He was one of the first Europeans to travel the entire length of the Mississippi River. His journeys allowed France to claim a vast part of North America for its empire.

La Salle was born in France in 1643. In his early twenties, he sailed to Canada and set up a fur-trading business. He explored the area around the Great Lakes and claimed large areas of land for France. The Indians told him about the Mississippi River. They believed it flowed into the sea.

La Salle decided to explore the Mississippi. In 1682, he led a group of about 20 Frenchmen and 30 Indians down the Illinois River and into the Mississippi in canoes. They reached the Gulf of Mexico on April 9, 1682, and La Salle claimed the Mississippi valley for France. He named the region Louisiana, in honor of King Louis XIV of France.

In 1684, La Salle sailed from France into the Gulf of Mexico. He wanted to land at the mouth of the Mississippi and start a colony there. But he landed in Texas by mistake. La Salle then led his men overland to the great river. When they could not find it, the men became angry and murdered La Salle.

See also **Mississippi River.**

laser

Light from a laser is powerful enough to drill a hole through the hardest diamond, yet precise enough to perform delicate eye surgery. Lasers are used to read a compact disk and the bar codes in a supermarket. Since its invention in the 1950s, the laser has become one of our most useful tools.

A laser makes a special kind of light. It gets its name from five words that describe how it makes this light. *Laser* stands for *l*ight *a*mplification by *s*timulated *e*mission of *r*adiation. All light is a form of energy, sometimes known as *radiation.* Usually, the light we see is a result of radiation that is *emitted*—released—in all directions. But the emissions of laser light are *stimulated*—triggered—by an energy source. This makes the laser light radiate in one direction only, concentrating the light energy. The laser light is also *amplified*—made stronger—by mirrors, much as the sound of a stereo is amplified by speakers. (*See* **light.**)

A laser has three important parts. The first is a *medium*—a solid, liquid, or gas that will release light when stimulated. The second part is an energy source. This stimulates the medium to emit light. The third part of a laser consists of two mirrors. The light bounces back and forth between the mirrors and becomes amplified. One of the mirrors does not reflect all of the light. It lets some of the light pass through, aiming the beam where it is desired.

A scientist monitors a strong laser in a laboratory.

The laser's power makes it suitable for many jobs in industry. Laser light can be used to cut, drill, or weld metals. It may also be used to carry telephone signals. One laser can send the signals for several hundred thousand telephone calls through glass "wires." And it can send the signals for all of these calls at the same time.

Because lasers may be beamed to objects so precisely, they can be used to detect tiny movements in the earth. Scientists use lasers in studying and predicting earthquakes. Lasers are also used in photography, and in a special kind of three-dimensional photography called *holography.*

Lasers are important in medicine, too. A laser may be used instead of a knife in surgery. Not only can it cut more precisely, but it can also prevent bleeding.

At left, an eye surgeon uses a laser beam to help repair damage in a patient's eye. At right, a laser reads product codes in a food market.

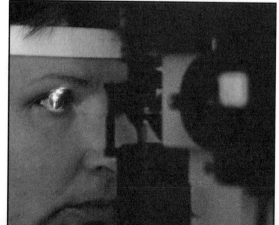

Latin America, *see* South America; Central America; West Indies; Mexico

latitude and longitude

On many maps, you will see a series of evenly spaced lines. Some run east and west. Others run north and south. These are lines of latitude and longitude. The lines do not actually exist on the earth. They are drawn on maps to help describe where a place is. They can help a ship's captain or an airplane pilot know in which direction to go. They can also help us understand and use maps.

Latitude On a globe, or on a flat map of the whole earth, you will see one line that runs around the middle of the earth. This line, halfway between the two poles, is called the *equator*. It is a line of latitude. Any place located right on the equator has a latitude of 0°. (*See* **equator**.)

The equator is also the line from which all other lines of latitude are measured. If a place is north of the equator, its latitude is measured in degrees north of the equator.

For example, the latitude of Chicago is about 42° N. The latitudes of places south of the equator are measured in degrees south of the equator. Sydney, Australia, has a latitude of 34° S.

The earth's most northern point is the North Pole. The most southern point is the South Pole. The North Pole is 90° north of the equator—latitude 90° N. The South Pole is 90° south of the equator—latitude 90° S.

Longitude The lines running north and south are the lines of longitude—also called *meridians*. The line from which longitude is measured is the Grand Meridian. The Grand Meridian runs from the North to the South poles. It passes through Great Britain and West Africa. Places to the west of the line have a west longitude. Places to the east have an east longitude. The lines of longitude meet at the poles.

Asia, Australia, and nearly all of Europe are in the east longitude. North and South America are in the west longitude. For example, Chicago is west of the Grand Meridian.

We can describe the location of the ship by its latitude and longitude. It is at 30° north latitude and 45° west latitude. Only one place on the globe has this "address." It is in the middle of the Atlantic Ocean, about halfway between North Africa and Florida.

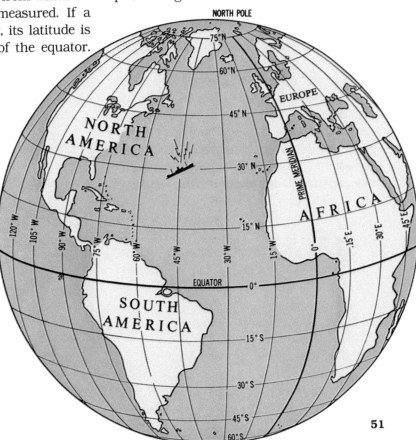

51

Its longitude is about 88° W. If you continue west, to the middle of the Pacific Ocean, you reach a line that is 180° W, exactly halfway around the world from the Grand Meridian. This line—called the *international dateline*—is also 180° E. (*See* **international dateline.**)

Each place on earth has its own latitude and longitude. If you know both measurements, you can find that place on a map. Other places may have the same latitude, and other places may have the same longitude. But no other place has *both* the same latitude and the same longitude.

Latter-Day Saints, *see* Mormons

Latvia, *see* Soviet Union

Laurier, Sir Wilfrid

Sir Wilfrid Laurier (LAW-rhee-ay) was the first French Canadian to become prime minister of Canada. He served in that office for 15 years, from 1896 until 1911. During this time, Canada was growing fast and trying to unite as one nation. Laurier gave Canada the strong leadership it needed.

Laurier was born in 1841 in St. Lin, Quebec, just north of the city of Montreal. Like most citizens of Quebec, Laurier spoke French as his first language. He learned English, too, because it is the language of most other Canadians. He studied law and started a law practice in 1864.

In 1871, Laurier was elected to Quebec's legislature. Three years later, he became a member of the Dominion Parliament, which made laws for all of Canada. Laurier worked hard to bring French Canadians and English Canadians together on national issues. In 1887, he became the leader of the Liberal party.

Laurier was elected prime minister in 1896. As prime minister, he encouraged immigrants to settle and farm Canada's vast western lands. He supported the building of

Sir Wilfrid Laurier was a great prime minister of Canada from 1896 to 1911.

railroads to link Canada's Atlantic and Pacific coasts. Laurier died in 1919.

See also **Canada.**

lava

Lava is rock that pours out of the earth in liquid form. At first, lava is very hot, and may flow like water. Then it cools and becomes like other kinds of rock.

Deep inside the earth, where temperatures are very high, there are pools of liquid rock called *magma.* Where magma finds a crack in the earth's surface, it may push up and pour out onto the land. When magma reaches the surface, it is called lava. While the lava is *molten*—liquid—it is so hot that it burns or melts whatever it touches. Lava is also the general name for the cooled rock that forms from molten lava.

As the lava cools, it forms different kinds of rock. Lava that still contains gases forms *pumice,* a light-colored rock full of tiny bubbles. Lava that cools very quickly forms a dark, glassy rock called *obsidian.* Most lava forms a dark, fine-grained rock called *basalt.*

Most lava pours out of a volcanic hole and builds up a volcanic mountain. Sometimes, lava flowing from cracks in the earth does not form a mountain. Some areas of the world are covered with lava beds—great sheets of rock. The lava beds in Washington State's Columbia Plateau are almost a mile thick.

Lava has been found on the moon and on Mars. On Mars, lava has formed huge volcanoes, much bigger than any on Earth.

See also volcano.

Lava shoots out of Mount Kilauea in Hawaii and runs downhill like water.

People who cannot settle a dispute (above) can ask a court to help settle it. Police can bring people who break laws to court.

law

A law is a rule made by the government of a city, state, or nation. Laws are passed to help people live together peacefully. They also protect each person's basic human rights. To make sure that laws are obeyed, governments punish people who break them.

There are two main kinds of law. *Civil law* helps settle disputes between people or companies. If someone thinks he or she has been wronged or injured by a person or company, he or she may *sue*—bring a lawsuit against that person or company. The court may order the person or company being sued to pay *damages*—a sum of money to make up for what has been lost or suffered. For example, a person hit by a car driven by a reckless driver may sue to make the driver pay medical bills.

Criminal law deals with *crimes*—actions that cause serious harm to an individual or a group. There are many kinds of crimes, ranging from shoplifting to murder. A person guilty of a crime is usually punished by having to spend time in jail. (*See* crime.)

A nation's laws are carried out by its *legal system.* An important part of this system is the police force. *Lawyers* also play a role in the legal system. A lawyer is a person who has studied law and passed a difficult test about laws. He or she is then permitted to give people advice about legal matters. For instance, when people buy a house, they pay a lawyer to make sure that the agreement they sign with the seller is correct.

Another part of the legal system consists of *courts*. These are places where a judge or a jury decides whether a law was broken. In the United States, a jury is usually a group of 12 citizens. They make their decision at the end of a trial. At a trial, people tell what they know about the incident. The judge or jury bases its decision on these reports.

A judge's decision can change future laws. For example, after a trial, a judge may decide that it is dangerous for a coal mine to employ workers under the age of 16. This decision means that all similar mines are forbidden to hire workers younger than 16.

Most cities, towns, and states have *legislatures*—groups of people elected to make laws. The U.S. Congress is the legislature for the whole nation. The main source of laws for the United States government is the U.S. Constitution.

See also **government; Congress, United States; Constitution of the United States;** and **Supreme Court, United States.**

lead

Lead is an element and a metal. It is blue-gray, soft, and very heavy. It is so heavy—twice as heavy as iron—that it is often used to stop X rays. Before X-raying your teeth, the dentist protects the rest of your body with a lead apron.

Today, most lead is used in car batteries. Lead is also used to make bullets, pipes, and tanks that hold sulfuric acid, and to make solder. Solder is an alloy of tin and lead. It is used to hold metals together and to fill cracks in metals. (*See* **alloy.**)

Lead used to be mixed in paint. Then people noticed that children who ate old paint chips or licked painted toys got sick. Even a small amount of lead can be harmful if you

eat it, breathe it, or absorb it through your skin. Lead can damage the brain, liver, and kidneys. Lead poisoning prevents the body from making healthy red blood cells.

Lead was added to gasoline to make it burn better. But the burned lead polluted the air and soil. Gasoline companies now make gasoline without lead.

Lead has been used for over 5,000 years. For a long time, people did not know it was poisonous. They made dishes and pipes from lead. In ancient Rome, the homes of rich people had lead plumbing. In fact, the word *plumbing* comes from *plumbum*, the Latin word for lead.

leaf

Leaves grow on trees and other plants. Even blades of grass are actually leaves of the grass plant. The leaves make food for plants and give off oxygen that animals need to breathe.

In a leaf, energy from sunlight, carbon dioxide from air, and water from soil combine to make food for the plant. This process is called *photosynthesis*. (*See* **photosynthesis.**)

Leaves are usually flat and thin. This shape makes them good collectors of sunlight. Veins run through each leaf, giving the leaf support. The veins also carry water and minerals to the food-making cells of the leaf. Then they carry the food away from the leaf to other parts of the plant.

If you look at a leaf through a microscope, you can see the cells that make up the leaf.

Seen through a microscope, the underside of a leaf has a network of veins.

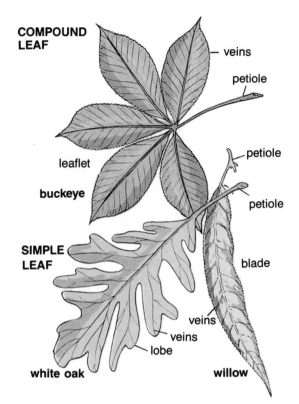

COMPOUND LEAF

veins

petiole

leaflet

buckeye

petiole

petiole

SIMPLE LEAF

blade

veins

veins

lobe

white oak

willow

A green material—*chlorophyll*—is in the leaf's food-making cells. Chlorophyll traps energy from sunlight and uses this energy to make food.

On the underside of the leaf, there are tiny openings. Carbon dioxide gas from the air enters the leaf through these openings. The leaf uses this gas and water to make its food. When a leaf makes food, it produces oxygen. The oxygen exits through the same tiny holes. This is the oxygen you breathe.

These tiny holes can open and close. Usually, they are open during the day and closed at night. But if it becomes very hot during the day, the holes close. This helps keep the leaf from losing water and drying out.

Leaves have another way to keep from drying out. Both sides of the leaf have a waxy covering. This covering keeps water inside the leaf.

Leaves come in many sizes, shapes, and textures. Leaves of pine trees are skinny needles. Grass has thin, bladelike leaves. A maple leaf is smooth, flat, and shaped like a hand. The leaves of a ginko tree look like small fans. A plant called "lamb's ears" has soft, furry leaves. The circular leaves of giant water lilies may grow to be 2 meters (6 feet)

The drawings above show the parts of a leaf. A *petiole* connects a leaf to the rest of the plant. *Veins* run toward the leaf edges. A compound leaf has several leaflets. A simple leaf is all one piece. Below, leaf shapes can help us recognize different plants.

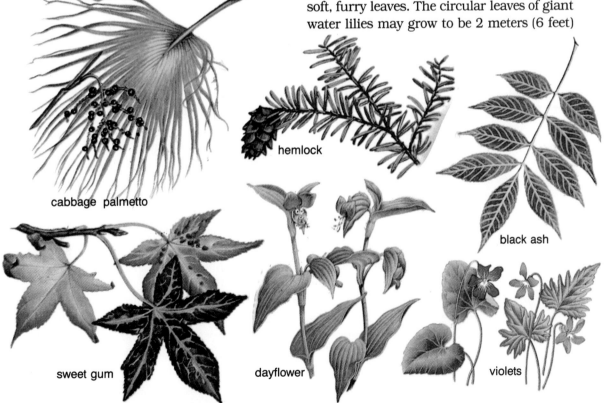

cabbage palmetto

hemlock

black ash

sweet gum

dayflower

violets

There are several kinds of learning. If you hit your thumb with a hammer (left), the pain helps you remember to be more careful next time. *Motor skills* such as roller skating (center) can be learned without using words. *Mental skills* such as playing a board game (right) require thinking and learning from experience.

across—and they can float. Leaves of a jade plant are thick and fleshy. They store water for the plant.

The leaves of some plants can do unusual things. The leaves of the sensitive plant respond to touch. If you touch them, they close up and droop. The leaves of Venus's-flytrap fold in the middle. When an insect lands on one, the leaf folds up and traps the visitor. The leaf then produces chemicals that digest the insect, so the plant can use it for food. The air plant has leaves with deep notches all along their edges. Baby plants grow from these notches. The tiny plants form leaves and roots. In time, the little plants get too heavy for the parent leaf. They drop off and land in the soil around the adult plant. There they take root and grow.

In temperate regions, leaves are green during spring and summer. The chlorophyll in the leaves gives them this color. But when chilly autumn begins, many leaves change color. Leaves have yellow, orange, red, or brown materials in them all the time. But these colors are hidden by the green chlorophyll. When the weather becomes cool, the chlorophyll breaks down. Then you see the other colors in leaves.

learning

Learning is knowledge gained by study or practice. Learning changes the way we behave. Most of the things we do are things we have learned to do. Some animals, too, may learn to do some things. But much animal behavior is not learned. It is done by instinct.

Human learning is more than what happens in school. Before children begin school, they learn to play, walk, and talk.

Some of the first things small children learn are *motor skills*—the use of their bodies. Crawling, walking, jumping, picking up objects, and opening and closing things are all motor skills. So is using a pencil to write. As a child grows, he or she can do more and more complicated things.

Children also begin to learn *mental skills* —skills that involve thinking. Recognizing shapes and understanding numbers are two mental skills. Reading is a very complicated mental skill.

A third kind of learning is the learning of *attitudes*—ways of thinking and feeling. We learn attitudes from people around us. If our parents like dogs, we may like dogs. Often, we do not know we are learning attitudes.

Some learning involves all three kinds. For example, in learning to play baseball, a person's body learns to bat, throw, and catch. A person's mind learns to plan where to run or where to throw the ball. The person also learns new attitudes needed to play a team game and deal with winning and losing.

Learning Problems Most children learn many kinds of skills quickly and easily. But not all children learn at the same rate. For example, if three children are learning to ice-skate, one may learn it very quickly, one after a little while, and one only after lots of practice and many falls. Children also learn mental skills at different rates. For some, this kind of learning is easy. For a few, it is very difficult. Children who learn slowly may have trouble with school subjects.

Scientists and teachers are learning about problems that children have with learning. Some slow learners may have a handicap due to an injury or an illness. Others may have problems with attitudes. For example, they may be very sad or angry about something that has happened to them. It is hard to learn when you are feeling sad or angry.

Children with learning problems often need special help from teachers and others. They also need the understanding of other students in their classes.

leather

Leather is made from animal skins. Most leather comes from the skins of beef cattle. Skins from goats, sheep, kangaroos, snakes, sharks, ostriches, and other animals are also made into leather. Thick skins are called *hides.* Thinner skins are called *skins.*

Most leather is made into shoes. Wallets, handbags, luggage, coats, belts, and other clothing may be made from leather. Leather is used for saddles and other equipment for horses. Once, most books were given leather bindings, and bookbinders sometimes still use leather.

Many steps are needed to turn animal skins into leather. The first step is salting them, which keeps them from rotting. Then they are sent to a *tannery,* a kind of leather factory.

At the tannery, the skins are soaked in water for about a day. Next, they are scraped to remove the flesh. Then they are soaked in chemicals that loosen any hair, and the hair is scraped off. After the next chemical bath, they start to show a *grain*—a pattern. Each kind of skin has its own grain.

The next step is *tanning.* The skin is soaked in a chemical made from minerals or vegetables. Once it is tanned the skin is called leather. Tanning makes the leather tough but flexible, so it can bend easily. Then a splitting machine makes the piece of leather an even thickness. The final step is *finishing.* Finishing can give the leather a color, pattern, or shiny appearance.

If all hair is removed, the outside of the leather is smooth. The inside is rough. It is called *suede.* For suede items—such as suede jackets and gloves—the rough side of the leather is made soft and fuzzy. If the hair is left on the skin, and the skin is not tanned, it is called *fur.* (*See* **fur.**)

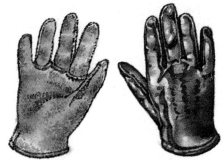

Suede (left) and leather (right) are the inside and the outside of an animal skin.

Leather was one of the first materials people learned how to use. Cave dwellers used skins for clothing. The earliest civilizations knew how to turn skins into leather.

Artificial leather does not come from animals. Most artificial leather today is made of a plastic called *vinyl.* It is used for shoes, handbags, and other items that are usually made from leather. Though vinyl may be made to look like leather, it is less expensive.

Lebanon

Capital: Beirut
Area: 4,015 square miles (10,400 square kilometers)
Population (1985): about 2,619,000
Official language: Arabic

Lebanon is a small Middle Eastern nation on the eastern shore of the Mediterranean Sea. Lebanon is about the size of Connecticut. It borders Israel in the south and Syria in the east and north.

Two mountain ranges run through Lebanon. The highest of the Lebanon Mountains is over 10,000 feet (3,500 kilometers) high. Many of the mountains are snow-covered in colder months. The Anti-Lebanon Mountains run along the eastern border with Syria. A narrow valley, the Bekaa, lies between the two ranges. This valley is one of the most fertile regions in the Middle East. Fruits are Lebanon's major farm products.

For many years, Lebanon was a popular place for tourists to visit. They enjoyed the dry, warm climate and beautiful Mediterranean beaches. Beirut, Lebanon's capital and main port, was a lively, modern city. Many people came to study Lebanon's rich history. But recently Lebanon has been torn by war. Few visitors come anymore.

About 5,000 years ago, Lebanon was home to the Phoenicians. They were a great sailing and trading nation and became a great

Lebanese who live in the countryside carry goods to market as their ancestors did 2,000 years ago.

power throughout the Mediterranean. Later, the Egyptians, the Babylonians, and the Persians ruled Lebanon. About 2,000 years ago, Lebanon was a part of the Roman Empire. Ancient Roman ruins can still be seen in parts of the Bekaa.

After the year 300, many Lebanese became Christians. Then, 300 years later, Arabs brought the new religion Islam to the region. Many Lebanese became Muslims, and Christians and Muslims often fought each other.

Lebanon first became an independent nation in 1943. About half of its people were Christian and the other half Muslim. Both Christian and Muslim leaders served in the government, yet they could not keep peace between their peoples. The two groups have been battling since the 1950s. Other nations have sent troops to keep order, but no one has been able to bring peace.

The Lebanese have suffered greatly from the wars. Factories and farms have been destroyed, and thousands of people have been killed. The peoples of Lebanon hope that someday peace will come, allowing them to rebuild their country.

See also **Islam** and **Christianity.**

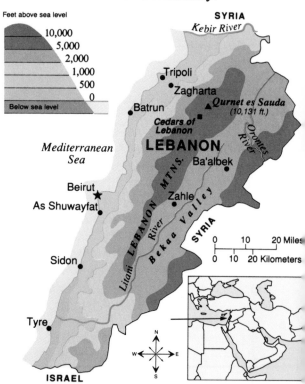

Robert E. Lee won battles for the South, but lost the war to stronger Union armies.

Lee, Robert E.

Robert E. Lee was commander of the Confederate Army during the American Civil War. Lee was respected by people in both the North and South. He remains one of the greatest military leaders in U.S. history.

Lee was born in 1807 to a wealthy Virginia family. His father, Henry, commanded a unit of horsemen during the Revolutionary War and was known as "Light-Horse Harry" Lee. Young Robert attended the U.S. Military Academy at West Point. He graduated second in his class, and married Martha Washington's great-granddaughter not long afterward. When the Civil War began in 1861, Lee was offered command of the Union forces. Not wishing to fight his friends and relatives in the South, he resigned from the U.S. Army. Returning home, Lee accepted command of the Army of Northern Virginia.

Lee led southern forces brilliantly throughout the war. He inspired his men to win nearly impossible victories. But in the end, the greater size and strength of the Union Army finally wore the South down. Lee surrendered in 1865.

No longer a soldier, Lee spent his last years as president of Washington College, in Virginia. When he died, in 1870, its name was changed to Washington and Lee University.

See also **Civil War** and **Confederate States of America.**

legend, *see* myths and legends

legislature, *see* government; Congress, United States

legume

Legumes make up one of the largest groups of flowering plants. There are over 14,000 kinds of legumes. They grow all over the world and supply food to many living things, including people. Peas, beans, clover, peanuts, and the locust tree all belong to the legume family.

All legumes produce their seeds in long pods. When you eat green beans or snow peas, you are eating the pods as well as the seeds. Legumes are a good source of protein.

The roots of legumes usually have bumps called *nodules.* Inside the nodules are bacteria so small you can see them only through

Legumes include many kinds of peas, beans, and clovers.

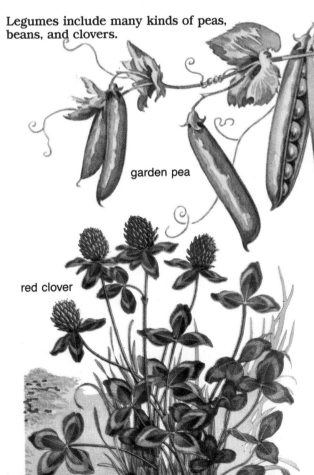

garden pea

red clover

a microscope. They are called *nitrogen-fixing bacteria.* They take nitrogen gas from the air and change it into solid nitrogen compounds.

Nitrogen is needed by all plants, not just legumes. That is why nitrogen is the main part of most fertilizers. Legumes are often planted in fields to fertilize the soil. If a farmer grows corn in the same field every season, the soil will run out of nitrogen. But if corn is planted one year and a legume—such as soybeans, clover, or alfalfa —the next, the soil will stay rich.

See also **nitrogen; beans and peas;** and **peanut.**

Leif Ericson, *see* Ericson, Leif

Lenin, V.I.

Lenin was a leader in the Russian Revolution, which brought communism to Russia in November 1917. Lenin and other members of the Bolshevik party took over the government by force. They renamed Russia the Russian Soviet Federated Socialist Republic. Later, it became the Soviet Union.

Lenin's real name was Vladimir Ilyich Ulyanov. He was born in a small town on the Volga River in 1870. He began signing the name Lenin to his writings in 1901. In the late 1800s, when he was growing up, Russia was a vast country ruled by a powerful king—the *czar.* Most Russians were very poor. Many wanted a new kind of government that would help the poor.

The czar's government did not like Lenin or others who wanted change. Lenin was thrown out of a university, spent time in jail, and lived abroad from 1907 until 1917.

In March 1917, revolutionaries overthrew the czar and tried to set up a democracy. But in November, Lenin returned to Russia. He and other Bolsheviks took over the government and established a communist system.

Lenin was a harsh ruler. He had many of his enemies put into prison or put to death.

Lenin speaks to a crowd in the early days of the Russian Revolution.

He planned to build the Soviet Union into a powerful country. But he died before his plans could be put in practice.

See also **Soviet Union** and **communism.**

lens

What do eyeglasses, binoculars, and your eyes have in common? They all contain one or more lenses. A lens is a piece of transparent material that is curved on one or both sides. A lens allows light rays to enter it. When light rays hit the lens, they slow down slightly. This change in speed changes their direction. So the light rays leave the lens headed in a slightly different direction. Depending on the shape of the lens, light rays will leave the lens closer together or farther apart.

If a lens bulges in the middle and is thinner on its edges, it is a *convex lens.* A convex lens changes the direction of light rays by

The *convex* lens bends light inward.
The *concave* lens bends the light outward.

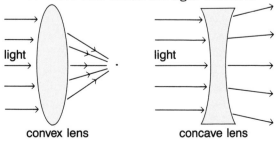
convex lens   concave lens

bringing them closer together. The point where the light rays come together is called the *focus.* A convex lens helps a farsighted person see things that are close.

Some lenses are *concave.* They are thinner in the middle than at the edges. This kind of lens spreads the light rays as they pass through the lens. A concave lens helps a nearsighted person see things that are at a distance.

See also **light.**

Leonardo da Vinci

Leonardo da Vinci was an amazing man of almost unlimited interests and talents. He was a scientist, an inventor, and a musician. Leonardo was also one of the world's most famous painters.

Leonardo was born in 1452 in the town of Vinci in Italy. His name means "Leonardo of Vinci." As a boy, he studied reading, writing, mathematics, and Latin. Like some other left-handed people, he wrote backward. His writing is easiest to read in a mirror.

Leonardo lived during a period known as the Renaissance. This was a time of renewed interest in art, science, and learning. Leonardo's father saw his son's artistic talent and sent him to the nearby city of Florence to study art. Leonardo learned about drawing shapes, about showing light and distance, and about colors. He began studying how the human body works. He sought knowledge from everyone. (*See* **Renaissance.**)

When he was about 25, Leonardo set up his own art studio. He carried a sketchbook wherever he went, but finished only about a dozen paintings. His painting called *The Last Supper* is one of the most famous in the world. It is painted on an inside wall of a monastery in Milan, Italy.

In 1503, Leonardo painted the *Mona Lisa,* a picture of a woman. For centuries, people have wondered what the woman is thinking and why she is smiling.

Leonardo was also known for his sculptures. But none of them have survived. In his spare time, he sang and played the lute. He also designed musical instruments. One was a wheeled drum that beat when it was pulled.

Leonardo designed military weapons, too. He came up with ideas for weapons that

Leonardo was a great scientist and inventor. He was also a great artist.

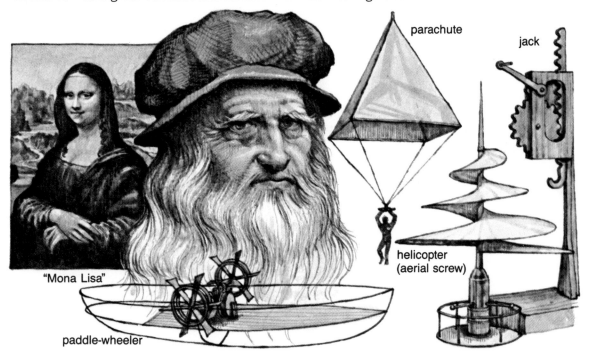

"Mona Lisa"

parachute

jack

helicopter (aerial screw)

paddle-wheeler

would not be built until hundreds of years later. He designed a tank, a machine gun, and a hand grenade.

Throughout his life, Leonardo observed nature very carefully. He studied plants, rocks, the flight of birds, the effects of sunlight and shadow, and the movements of water. Among the hundreds of things he worked on were ideas for flying machines, an explanation of how mirrors work, and the invention of a life preserver.

In 1517, King Francis I of France invited Leonardo to move to his country. Leonardo died in France on May 2, 1519. He left notebooks filled with ideas that no one else would dream of for hundreds of years.

Lesotho, *see* Africa

Lewis and Clark Expedition

From 1804 to 1806, the Lewis and Clark expedition explored the huge frontier west of the Mississippi River. The United States had just bought a large area of land from France—the Louisiana Purchase. President Thomas Jefferson wanted to encourage Americans to settle the new land. But first, there was much to learn about it. Jefferson decided to send a team to explore it.

Jefferson chose two men to lead the expedition. One was his private secretary, Meriwether Lewis, and the other was Lewis's friend William Clark. Lewis and Clark had served as army officers. Both were experienced frontiersmen, and Clark knew how to draw maps. They selected 40 men to go with them. They chose men who knew Indian languages and who knew how to live in the wilderness.

Jefferson wanted the explorers to follow the Missouri River to its source in the Rocky Mountains. They would then cross the Rockies and follow the Columbia River. Jefferson hoped the expedition would find a water route to the Pacific Ocean. Along the way, the explorers were to learn about the Indians and make friends with them. They also were to study the land's plant and animal life.

In May 1804, the expedition set out from St. Louis, Missouri. They traveled up the

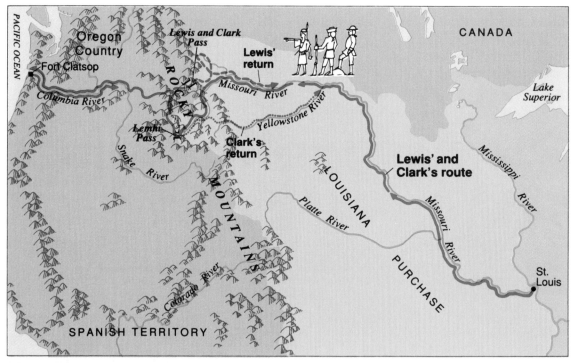

Missouri River. Supplies ran low, and a few boats sank. But the explorers were amazed at the variety of animals and the beauty of the land. An Indian woman, Sacagawea, guided them part of the way. She also acted as their interpreter when they met Indians.

The expedition made it to the source of the Missouri. It took a month to walk the narrow paths through the Rockies. Then the explorers built new canoes and paddled down the Columbia River. In November 1805, Lewis and Clark arrived at the Pacific Ocean.

By the time the group returned to St. Louis, in the fall of 1806, they had traveled almost 7,700 miles (12,400 kilometers). Jefferson was very pleased, and carefully studied the maps and reports they brought back. They learned a great deal that would help Americans settle the West. Their trip along the Columbia River also gave the United States a claim to the Oregon Territory, rich in furs and farmland.

See also **Louisiana Purchase; westward movement; Jefferson, Thomas; Sacagawea;** and **explorers.**

Liberia, *see* Africa

Liberty Bell

"Proclaim Liberty throughout all the Land unto all the Inhabitants thereof." These words are on the Liberty Bell. It is no longer rung, because it is cracked. But the bell is still a symbol of freedom to Americans.

The Liberty Bell was made in England in 1752, during American colonial days. A British bellmaker cast the 2,000-pound (900-kilogram) bell, then shipped it to Philadelphia. It was hung in the Pennsylvania state house—now called Independence Hall. (*See* **Independence Hall.**)

People were eager to test the new bell. But when they rang it, the bell cracked. Workers recast the bell, and again it cracked. Recast once more, it was hung in the State House *belfry*—bell tower.

The Liberty Bell is a symbol of American independence.

When the Declaration of Independence was read in July 1776, every bell in Philadelphia, including the state house bell, rang to celebrate. During the Revolutionary War, Americans hid the bell. They did not want the British to melt it down to make bullets.

The Liberty Bell cracked the last time in 1835, when it was rung for the death of Chief Justice John Marshall. Today, it is in Philadelphia's Liberty Bell Pavilion. It is still struck on very special occasions.

See also **Declaration of Independence** and **Revolutionary War.**

library

A library is a place where books, magazines, phonograph records, and other sources of information are kept. Libraries are organized so people can use them easily. Some libraries fill huge buildings. Other libraries are so small that they fit in a single room. Specially trained people called *librarians* manage libraries and help people find what they are looking for.

Kinds of Libraries Many countries have *public libraries.* In the United States, public libraries are run by towns and cities. Anyone who lives in the town can get a library card and borrow books.

Libraries keep books on many interesting subjects (above). They also have films, recordings, and information available by computer.

Most public libraries are *general libraries.* They have all kinds of books and other materials for study or for fun. A general library will have a section just for children, or sometimes a children's room.

In larger cities, the public library usually has many branches. Some branches may be *special libraries.* One special library may be for children. It will have books, magazines, and records that children enjoy. Both general and children's libraries often have "story hours"—times when a librarian reads stories aloud. Some also show movies and videotapes.

Other special libraries may collect printed and recorded music. Some have braille books and recorded tapes for the blind. (*See* **braille.**)

Another kind of special library is a *research library.* People studying a subject very carefully use a research library. Many of the books in a research library can be read only at the library. They cannot be borrowed to read at home.

How Libraries are Organized A library has a *catalog* of all its books, magazines, records, and other materials. It tells you where in the library to find all these things. In some libraries, the catalog is a set of card files. In others, the catalog is a set of books. Some library catalogs are on a computer. You type in the name of a book, author, or subject. The computer tells you whether the library has that book, or any books by that author or about that subject.

Most newspapers and magazines now come to libraries on *microfilm* as well as on paper. One roll of microfilm has tiny photographs of each newspaper page. To read the film, you run it through a microfilm reader. It makes each tiny photograph large enough to read. Libraries may also have copies of hard-to-get books on microfilm.

The History of Libraries The earliest libraries did not have any books. They had clay tablets with writing scratched onto them. These libraries were owned by kings in ancient Mesopotamia, in the Middle East.

In Roman times, books were scrolls (above). Below, a horse-drawn traveling library brought books to people around 1900.

The most famous ancient library was in Alexandria, Egypt. It had a copy of all known written works—as many as 700,000. They were on *scrolls*—long rolls—of *papyrus,* an early kind of paper. But all the scrolls in the library were destroyed by fire and war.

During the Middle Ages—from about 500 to 1300—most libraries in Europe were in monasteries. Monks studied the books and wrote out copies of them. After 1400, rich families began to collect books for their own libraries. After Johannes Gutenberg invented movable type, around 1450, it cost less to print books. More people had books. Universities gathered large collections. (*See* **Gutenberg, Johannes.**)

In 1638, John Harvard started the first library in the United States by giving his books to what is now Harvard University. The country's first free public library began in 1833 in Peterborough, New Hampshire. The Library of Congress—created in 1800 —is now one of the world's largest.

See also **books.**

Libya

Capital: Tripoli
Area: 679,359 square miles (1,759,540 square kilometers)
Population (1985): about 3,752,000
Official language: Arabic

Libya is a large country on the northern coast of Africa. It is bigger than the state of Alaska. But most of Libya is covered by the hot, dry Sahara Desert.

Very few people live in Libya's desert regions. A few live near *oases*—small areas made fertile by underground water. But most of Libya's people live along the Mediterranean coast in the north. Tripoli, Libya's capital, and other large cities are on the northern coast. Libya's good farming regions are also in the north. Even there, farmers grow crops that require little rain. These crops include fruit and wheat.

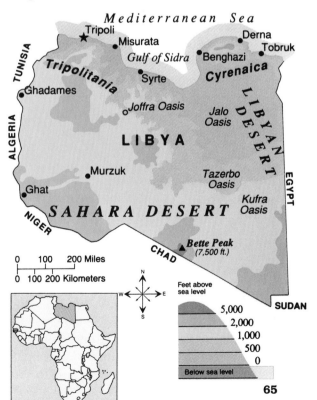

Libya's hot, dry climate is good for growing oranges and other fruits.

Most Libyans are Arabs, like the peoples of other countries in North Africa and the Middle East. The first settlers in the region were Berbers, natives of northern Africa. The Berbers moved into Libya more than 3,000 years ago.

Libya has been part of great empires. In the centuries before Christ, Carthage, a powerful city-state, controlled much of northern Africa, including Libya. When Carthage was conquered by the Roman Empire, Libya came under Roman rule.

After the prophet Muhammad founded Islam in the middle 600s, Libya became part of the Arab world. Libyans became Muslims—followers of Islam.

Arab customs and Islam are very important in Libyan life today. Almost all Libyans live according to the laws and traditions of Islam. Under Islamic law, for example, women have few rights. Punishment for crimes can be very harsh. For example, a criminal might be beaten in public.

Libya was a poor nation until oil was discovered there in the 1950s. Then the government became very rich by selling oil to other countries. Scientists believe that Libya still has billions of barrels of oil underground.

In 1969, a dictator named Muammar el-Qadaffi (kuh-DAH-fee) seized control of the government. His policies angered many other nations, including the United States. *See also* **Islam.**

lichen

A lichen (LY-kun) is two living things in one, part fungus and part alga. Most kinds of fungi and algae live in warm, moist places. But when a fungus and an alga join and form a lichen, they can live where it is cold and dry. Lichens can even live in the Arctic. (*See* **fungus** and **algae.**)

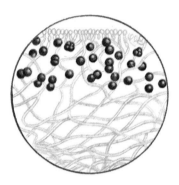

Above, in a lichen, the stringy fungi protect the green beads of algae. Algae make food for themselves and the fungus. Below, two common lichens—speckled lichen on a tree, and scale lichen on a rock.

speckled lichen   scale lichen

The two parts of a lichen help each other stay alive. The fungus makes a cover that helps keep the alga from drying out. The alga can make its own food. It feeds itself and feeds the fungus, too. When two different life forms help each other live, we say that they are *symbiotic*. (*See* **symbiosis.**)

Old-man's-beard (right) is a lichen that hangs from tree branches. Reindeer moss (below) is an important food for reindeer and caribou in the Arctic. British soldiers (bottom) have red caps just as the soldiers once did.

old-man's beard

reindeer moss

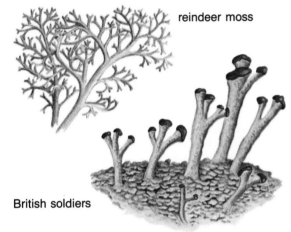

British soldiers

Lichens come in different shapes and colors. Some look like orange or yellow crusts growing on rocks. Some look like tiny gray leaves on rocks, trees, or soil. Others look like little shrubs. A shrublike lichen, reindeer moss, grows in Arctic regions. In winter, it is an important food for reindeer and caribou.

Most lichens grow very slowly. During a human lifetime, they may grow only a few millimeters. But lichens can live for a long time. Some are more than 4,000 years old!

Liechtenstein, *see* Europe

---

life cycle

Every living thing begins life and then grows, reproduces, and dies. Different living things have different ways of growing and reproducing. The series of changes a living thing goes through in its life is called its *life cycle.* Biologists better understand living things by studying their life cycles.

Some living things have very short life cycles. A single bacterium may live and grow for only 20 minutes. Then it divides into two new bacteria. After another 20 minutes, these two bacteria each divide, and there are four. Other living things have much longer life cycles. Elephants and humans may live 80 years or more. Some trees live hundreds or even thousands of years.

Simple Life Cycles Some living things have simple life cycles. Others have life cycles that involve more changes.

A seed-bearing plant has a simple life cycle. Its life begins when a seed sprouts and begins to grow. The young plant soon looks like the plant that produced the seed. When the plant is grown, it, too, produces seeds. Some of these seeds sprout and produce new plants all over again. Some seed-bearing plants die after a single summer. Others, such as trees, may live for years.

Many animals, too, have simple life cycles. These life cycles begin when eggs made by females are fertilized by sperm made by males. A fertilized egg grows into a small animal that looks very much like its parents. The small animal grows until it is old enough to produce eggs or sperm itself. Snakes, birds, cats, and humans have this kind of life cycle.

Complex Life Cycles Frogs and other amphibians have *complex* life cycles. They must go through extra stages before they finally look like adults. Adult female frogs mate and lay eggs in water. The eggs develop into tiny swimming animals called *tadpoles.* A tadpole is a frog, but it looks like a tiny fish. It has a tail and fins for swimming. It has gills so it can breathe in water. It cannot live on land. (*See* **larva.**)

As the tadpole grows, its body changes. It grows legs in place of fins. Its tail disappears. It becomes able to breathe air and live on land. Soon, it is an adult frog. In time, it will produce offspring and start the cycle again. (*See* **amphibian.**)

Butterflies have a complex life cycle, too. A butterfly lays its eggs on a plant. From an

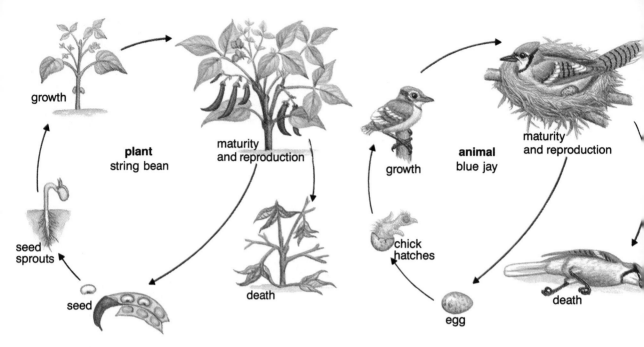

Reproduction is a necessary part of the life cycle. A plant makes seeds that sprout into new plants. A bird lays eggs from which baby birds will hatch.

egg comes a tiny wormlike animal called a *caterpillar*. It has no wings and does not look at all like an adult butterfly. For weeks, it eats and grows fat. (*See* **caterpillar.**)

Then the caterpillar attaches itself to a branch by a thread. It covers itself with a hard case called a *chrysalis*. It has made itself into a *pupa*. Inside the chrysalis, the insect's whole body changes. The pupa becomes an adult butterfly.

When the chrysalis splits open, the insect comes out and unfolds its beautiful wings. It is a fully formed butterfly! One day, the butterfly will lay eggs and start a new life cycle. Then it will die. (*See* **butterflies and moths.**)

Plants can have complex life cycles, too. For example, mosses have three stages in their life cycle. In the first stage, the moss is a tiny *spore*. From the spore sprouts a green moss plant—the second stage. The green plant produces eggs and sperm. When an egg and sperm join, they form a fertilized egg. The egg grows into a brown stalk with a knob on the end—the third stage. The knob is a case in which hundreds of spores form. When the spores are ripe, the case breaks open. The spores are carried by the wind to new places, where they sprout. (*See* **mosses and liverworts.**)

light

Have you ever seen the brilliant colors of fireworks light up the night sky? Maybe you have seen the start of a new day as the sun's glowing light comes up over the horizon. Whether by dazzling sunlight or by the glow of firelight, we need light to see. Light is a form of energy that we can detect with our eyes.

The Nature of Light Many scientists have tried to describe light. If you are in strong sunlight, you can tell from its heat that light is a form of energy. Scientists have used two different ideas to explain light. One idea is that light is a form of energy that travels in waves. The other idea is that light travels in little bundles or particles, called *photons*.

Most of the time it is easier to think of light as waves. If light travels in waves, we can explain why light does most of what we see it doing. On the other hand, a few things can be explained only by thinking of light as particles. Scientists say that light is a wave and a particle at the same time.

Light waves are like ripples that move away in all directions from a source. Think of what happens when a pebble is thrown into a still pond. Waves form around the disturbance in the water. The waves go out in all directions. We can think of light this way, too.

How Light Travels Light travels extremely fast. It can go from the earth to the moon and back in about 3 seconds. Light travels about 300,000 kilometers (186,000 miles) per second through empty space. Light from the sun takes 8 minutes to reach us on the earth. When light travels through a medium such as air or glass, it slows down just a little. But to our eyes, light seems to travel in almost no time at all. (*See* **light-year.**)

As a beam of light travels away from its source, it gradually becomes weaker and weaker. Imagine shining a flashlight into a dark cave. The light may be very bright shining on a near wall. But when you shine the light toward the back of the cave, the light becomes very weak. As light waves move away from the source, they spread out in all directions. Over a long distance, this spreads the light over a great area. The light in any one place in that area is too weak to be seen.

Shining a light on a nearby surface lights a small area. Shining a light on a distant surface sheds light over a larger area.

Light Is Electromagnetic Radiation
Light results from two kinds of energy that are very closely related—electric energy and magnetic energy. Moving together, they create a wave that is part electric and part magnetic. That is why scientists call light *electromagnetic radiation.*

But not all electromagnetic radiation is alike. The light that we see is only one kind of electromagnetic radiation. Electromagnetic waves have different *wavelengths* —sizes. Some waves are very small, while others are large. The waves that our eyes can detect are called *visible light.* Some forms of electromagnetic radiation with wavelengths that we cannot see are X rays and microwaves, which have short wavelengths. We also cannot see radio waves, which are very long.

Because light is electromagnetic, it is related to electrons—the tiny charged particles found in atoms. When an electron loses energy, it releases light. Fires and light bulbs produce light because they use heat to increase the energy of electrons. Then, as the electrons lose some of that extra energy, they release light. (*See* **lights and lighting** and **atom.**)

Light and Matter When you see something, light has traveled through the air to your eyes, into your pupils, and through the lenses of your eyes. When light can easily pass through a material, we say the material is *transparent.* Air and glass are transparent. Other materials, such as waxed paper, let only some light pass through. Those are called *translucent.* Some materials, such as bricks, will not let any light pass through. Those materials are called *opaque.*

1. *Transparent* materials let most light through so that we can see what is on the other side.
2. *Translucent* materials let some light through.
3. *Opaque* materials let no light through.

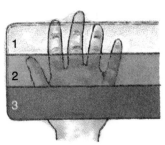

Like a ball hitting a wall, a ray of light that strikes a mirror bounces back. It is *reflected* by the mirror. Light is always reflected at the same angle at which it struck. That is why we see ourselves in a mirror. It is also why a setting sun makes a pond glow with reflected sunlight. Even our moon, which produces no light of its own, glows at night with the light it reflects from the sun.

Did you ever put a pencil in a glass of water and notice that it looks crooked in the water? That shows another interesting thing about light. Light bends when it goes from one material or medium to another. Light travels at one speed in air. But it slows down just a little when it enters water. This change causes the light to bend slightly when it enters the water. The bending of light is called *refraction.*

Each different color of light bends by different amounts. When a ray of light enters a glass prism or a crystal, the different colors become separate. Seeing the separate colors, we realize that white light is made from all the colors of the rainbow. The rainbow-colored pattern is called the *spectrum* of white light. (*See* **rainbow.**)

Using Light Since light is a form of energy, it can do work. Many modern inventions use the power of light. Solar cells change the sun's radiant energy into electricity. These depend on the particle nature of light. So do the detectors—sometimes called *electric eyes*—that can "see" an opaque object, such as a person.

We also use light in other special ways. Messages can be sent by light signals. Today, extremely short blips of light carry telephone conversations through thin strands of glass called *optical fibers.* Scientists hope to build better computers and other electronic devices that use light instead of electricity.

lighthouse

As a ship nears shore, it faces many dangers. It can be torn open by sharp rocks and reefs under the surface of the water. It can get stuck in shallow water. It can be caught in powerful currents or flipped over by huge waves crashing into shore. For centuries, people have built lighthouses—tall towers with bright lights on them—to warn ships about such dangers. A lighthouse is built

A mirror *reflects* light. Standing in front of it, we can see ourselves.

light

mirror surface

reflection

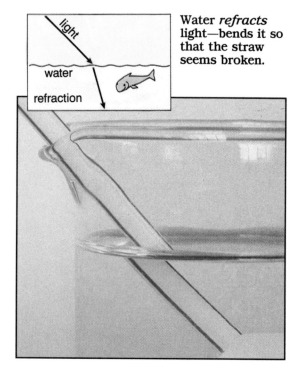

Water *refracts* light—bends it so that the straw seems broken.

light

water

refraction

The brilliant light in a lighthouse helps ships avoid dangerous rocks at night.

near or actually on the dangerous area. Most lighthouses also have foghorns. During heavy fog, sailors hear the horn even if they cannot see the light.

In 280 B.C., king Ptolemy II of Egypt had a gigantic lighthouse built on Pharos, an island in the Bay of Alexandria. At night, a huge fire burning atop the Pharos lighthouse could be seen from miles away. This lighthouse was known as one of the Seven Wonders of the World until an earthquake destroyed it in the 1300s. (*See* **Alexandria.**)

Lighthouses have burned candles, oil, and gas lamps. Today's lighthouses use powerful electric lights, made even brighter by reflectors and lenses. They are thousands of times brighter than the lighthouse at Pharos.

lightning

The sky becomes dark, and a thunderstorm is on the way. Suddenly, a flash lights up the sky. Moments later, a deep sound rolls across the land. The flash is lightning, and the deep rumble is thunder. Lightning strikes somewhere on Earth about 100 times each second.

What is lightning? It is a huge spark of electricity in a thundercloud. A cloud has positive charges in some parts and negative charges in others. Like magnets, the positive and negative charges attract each other. When the attraction is strong enough, a huge negative charge of electrons suddenly jumps to wherever the positive charges are—in the same cloud, another cloud, or the ground.

We see flashes of lightning in different forms. *Forked lightning* zigzags through the air on two or more paths. The leader strikes the ground or a high object, and side forks fizzle and die. As the leader strikes downward, a return stroke jumps back upward into the sky. *Sheet* or *heat lightning* appears as a curtain of lightning. It is really ordinary lightning seen from a great distance, often with its light reflected by clouds.

Lightning can be very dangerous. It can damage buildings. It can injure or kill trees, animals, or people. If you are caught in a thunderstorm, crouch down in a low place away from trees or water. Lightning is attracted to water and tall objects, such as trees, steeples, and utility poles.

See also **electricity** and **thunderstorm.**

Lightning strikes tall objects. Taking shelter under a tree can be dangerous!

lightning bug, *see* firefly

lights and lighting

Light lets us see things. When we are outdoors during the day, the light we use is sunlight. At night, we can see by moonlight. Moonlight is really sunlight that is *reflected* —bounced—off the moon.

Early Forms of Lighting Very early humans had only light from the sun and moon. After they discovered fire, they had light from fire, too. For hundreds of years, fires were the main source of lighting at night. People learned how to control fire to improve lighting. For example, they made wax candles and oiled torches. They made lamps of stone and clay, filled them with oil, and put a burning wick in the oil. They put the burning wick inside a glass lantern to keep the flame from blowing out. Fires in fireplaces provided light as well as heat.

By the 1800s, people had turned to different fuels to provide lighting. Natural gas or gas made from coal was burned in streetlamps and in many homes and workplaces. Kerosene, a fuel made from petroleum, was burned in small lamps.

Candles are still used today for lighting. So are fires in fireplaces and kerosene lamps. But none of these is an important source of lighting any more. Electric lighting is, by far, the main source of lighting in the modern world.

The lamps and overhead lights in your home are electric. So are the lights in offices, factories, and stores. Street lights are electric, too. Even most portable lights are electric. A flashlight, for example, gets its electricity from batteries. (*See* **battery.**)

Electric lights were first invented in the 1870s. Thomas Edison invented a long-lasting electric light bulb in 1879. After that, electric lights were widely used. By the 1920s in the United States, electricity was the power behind most lighting. (*See* **Edison, Thomas Alva.**)

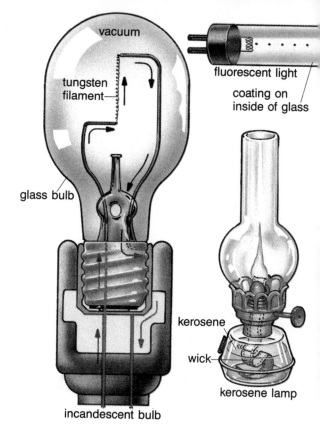

vacuum

fluorescent light

coating on inside of glass

tungsten filament

glass bulb

kerosene

wick

kerosene lamp

incandescent bulb

Kinds of Lighting Today there are several ways of producing electric light. Most light we use is produced by incandescent (in-can-DESS-ent) light bulbs. Electricity flows through a *filament*—a tiny piece of wire—inside the bulb. The electricity heats the filament. The filament does not catch fire, because there is no air inside the bulb. Instead, it glows, like the flame of a candle, producing light.

The amount of electricity used by a light bulb to produce light is measured in watts. A 60-watt bulb may provide enough light to read by. A more powerful bulb is used to light up an entire room. A 75-watt, 100-watt, or 150-watt bulb may be used. Bulbs with an even higher number of watts are used where very bright light is needed. For example, a photographer may need to shine a very bright light on the person or object being photographed. A doctor doing surgery also needs very bright light.

Many homes, offices, schools, and factories use fluorescent (fluhr-ESS-ent) lights. A fluorescent light does not use a heated filament to produce light. A fluorescent light is a glass tube filled with gas. When electricity flows

gas
be

neon light

A kerosene lamp produces light with a flame. Incandescent, fluorescent, neon, and mercury-vapor lights produce stronger light with electricity.

through the tube, the gas gives off ultraviolet light. This light causes the coating on the bulb to glow.

A fluorescent light uses less electricity than an incandescent bulb. Using the same number of watts, it can produce three times as much light. That is the main reason fluorescent lights are used to light larger spaces. They also last longer.

Mercury-vapor or *sodium-vapor* lighting is another kind of lighting. Electricity flows through a gas—a *vapor*—in a glass container and causes the gas to glow. Mercury-vapor or sodium-vapor lights are often used outdoors. They may be used for lighting streets or highways, or even to light whole stadiums for nighttime sports events.

Street and highway lighting makes the world safer. Highway lighting helps prevent car accidents. Street lighting helps to prevent crime.

Some lights are used for their color. *Neon* lights, for example, bring glowing colors to the night world. Like mercury-vapor lights or sodium-vapor lights, neon lights use electricity to light up a gas in a tube. At first, they used only neon, a gas that produced a

bright orange light. Other gases are used today to make other colors, but they are still called neon lights. Many stores, movie theaters, and restaurants use colorful neon light for their signs. (*See* **neon.**)

See also **electricity.**

light-year

A light-year is the distance that light travels in one year. Astronomers use the light-year as a unit of measure, just as we use a kilometer or a mile. A light-year is for very long distances.

How much distance does a light-year cover? It is difficult for most people to imagine. Suppose that at noon on your ninth birthday, you sent a flash of light out into space. For the next twelve months, that burst of light would be traveling through space. Every second, it would travel 300,000 kilometers (186,000 miles). Finally, at noon on your tenth birthday, the light would reach the other end of a light-year. The light would be 9,460,000,000,000 kilometers (5,878,000,000,000 miles) away from you!

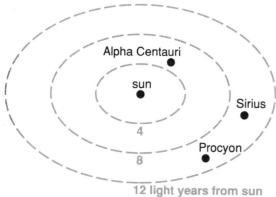

Stars near the solar system are more than five light-years away—trillions of miles!

Astronomers have to use long measurements like this to measure the great distances between stars and galaxies. In fact, to an astronomer, a light-year is not very far. The star nearest the sun is about 4 light-years away, and the nearest galaxy to the sun is about 170,000 light-years away. (*See* **galaxy**.)

limerick

A limerick is a short, funny poem. All limericks have five lines. The last words of the first, second, and last lines all rhyme. The last words of the third and fourth lines rhyme. You can see how this works in this limerick by Edward Lear:

There was a young lady whose chin
Resembled the point of a pin.
She had it made sharp,
And purchased a harp,
And played several tunes with her chin.

A limerick always has a ONE-two-three, ONE-two-three rhythm. In lines 1, 2, and 5, there are three *stresses*—words or syllables said with extra force. Lines 3 and 4 have two stresses. Here is the same limerick with the stressed words in capital letters.

There WAS a young LA-dy whose CHIN
Re-SEM-bled the POINT of a PIN.
She HAD it made SHARP,
And PUR-chased a HARP,
And PLAYED several TUNES with her CHIN.

Here is a limerick that is also a tongue twister.

A tutor who tooted the flute
Tried to tutor two tooters to toot.
Said the two to the tutor,
"Is it harder to toot or
To tutor two tooters to toot?"

limestone

Limestone is a kind of rock found throughout the world. It is a *sedimentary rock*. Sedimentary rock forms from materials that collect at the bottom of a body of water. Shale and sandstone are also sedimentary rocks.

Most limestone forms on the floor of a warm, shallow sea or ocean. Limestone is made of the skeletons or shells of animals that lived in these seas. It may be formed from the skeletons of corals, or from the shells of oysters and clams. It also may be formed from the shells of *foraminifera*. These animals are so small that you need a microscope to see them. When these creatures die, their tiny skeletons and shells sink to the seafloor. Over thousands of years, they pile up to form thick layers called *deposits*.

Limestone—made from millions of shells—was formed in layers deep under the earth.

After millions of years, these thick deposits turn to rock—limestone. When we find limestone on dry land, we know that the area was once covered by ocean.

Rain water can seep into limestone deposits. In some places, it has dissolved large openings in the limestone, forming caves and tunnels. Sometimes, rivers flow through these tunnels.

See also **marble.**

Lincoln, Abraham

Abraham Lincoln was the 16th president of the United States. He was president during the Civil War.

Abe was born in a log cabin near Hodgenville, Kentucky, on February 12, 1809. He was the second child, after his sister Sarah, born to Tom and Nancy Hanks Lincoln.

The Lincolns were hardworking pioneers. They moved frequently, always looking for a better farm. When Abe was seven, the Lincolns moved to Indiana. They arrived just before winter and put up a "half-faced camp." It had three walls. The fourth side, away from the wind, stood open. A fire burned all the time during the cold winter. In the spring, neighbors helped the Lincolns build a more solid, four-sided log cabin. One wall had a row of pegs. Each night, Abe climbed up these pegs to his sleeping loft under the roof.

Abe and Sarah had to work on the farm, so they usually could not go to school. In fact, Lincoln later said he had only a year's schooling. But even without school, Abe learned quickly. He liked to read and would walk miles to borrow books. He amazed neighbors with how much he knew.

When Abe was eight, he was given an ax and taught how to use it. For many years, he used the ax to split logs into rails for building houses and fences.

Abe's mother died when he was nine. A year later, Abe's father married Sarah Bush Johnston, a widow with three children. She was a loving mother to the Lincoln children.

She encouraged Abe in his learning. He grew strong and tall. By the time Abe was 20, he was 6 feet, 4 inches tall.

When Abe turned 21, his family moved again, this time to Illinois. By now, he was old enough to be on his own. He decided to float a flatboat loaded with cargo down the Mississippi River to New Orleans. Months later, he returned north to settle in New Salem, Illinois. He opened a store, but it failed. Then he became a surveyor, measuring plots of land in the new state.

Lincoln thought of himself as "a piece of floating driftwood" during this time. But his honesty, friendliness, and storytelling made him very popular in New Salem. In 1834, he was elected to the Illinois legislature. That same year, he began borrowing lawbooks and reading them in his spare time. In two years, he became a lawyer.

In 1837, Lincoln moved to Springfield, the new state capital. He practiced law, and also met Mary Todd. They married in 1842 and had four sons. But only the oldest, Robert Todd Lincoln, lived to adulthood.

Abe Lincoln grew up in a log cabin that had a crude loft for sleeping.

Lincoln, Abraham

Lincoln became a U.S. congressman in 1847. He served one term, then returned to his law practice in Illinois. But the slavery issue caused him to go back into politics in 1858. He ran for the U.S. Senate, wanting to stop the spread of slavery into new states and territories. He and his opponent, Senator Stephen A. Douglas, debated each other seven times. Douglas won the election, but Lincoln gained national fame for his stand against slavery.

Two years later, Lincoln ran for president. Upset about Lincoln's views on slavery, the southern states threatened to *secede*—withdraw—from the United States if he was elected. When Lincoln won the election, the southern states left the Union and formed the Confederate States of America. The Civil War began in April 1861, a month after Lincoln became president.

The war years were very hard for President Lincoln. People blamed him when the North

This photograph of Lincoln was used for the engraving on the five-dollar bill.

lost battles. He was deeply hurt by the great loss of life on both sides. People said his Kentucky-born wife favored the Confederate side. Lincoln missed his son Willie, who had died from typhoid.

Lincoln meets with officers of the Union Army after the battle of Antietam in 1862. He was 6 feet, 4 inches tall, and his stovepipe hat made him look even taller.

But Lincoln trusted that he was doing the right thing. In January 1863, he issued a document called the Emancipation Proclamation. He declared that all slaves, even those in the Confederate States, would be free. This action helped end slavery in the United States.

At a cemetery for soldiers killed at Gettysburg, Pennsylvania, Lincoln made a three-minute speech. This simple but beautiful speech is remembered as the Gettysburg Address. (*See* **Gettysburg.**)

Near the end of the war, Union victories helped Lincoln win a second term as president. He urged the North to treat the South kindly and "bind up the nation's wounds." The war ended on April 9, 1865.

Five days later, Lincoln and his wife went to see a play at Ford's Theatre in Washington, D.C. As they watched from a balcony, a man named John Wilkes Booth crept up behind them. He shot Lincoln in the head. Then he leaped down onto the stage and ran away.

Lincoln died the next morning, April 15, 1865. A funeral train carried him slowly home to Illinois. People stood weeping by the railroad tracks the whole way.

See also **Civil War** and **slavery.**

Lincoln was assassinated—killed—while watching a play. John Wilkes Booth, the assassin, was later caught and hanged.

Charles Lindbergh stands in front of his famous plane, the *Spirit of St. Louis.*

Lindbergh, Charles

Charles Lindbergh—"Lucky Lindy"—was the first person to fly alone across the Atlantic Ocean without stopping.

Lindbergh was born in Detroit, Michigan, in 1902. Before he was two years old, the first airplane was flown successfully. As a boy, he dreamed of learning to fly. In 1922, he went to flying school. For the next two years, he traveled around the country, doing daredevil airplane stunts at fairs. He was also one of the first pilots to carry the U.S. mail.

In 1926, Lindbergh heard about a $25,000 prize for the first person to fly nonstop across the Atlantic. He asked a group of businessmen from St. Louis, Missouri, to pay for a plane. He named his plane the *Spirit of St. Louis* in their honor.

On a cloudy, wet morning—May 20, 1927—Lindbergh took off from New York City. He landed near Paris 33 hours later, on May 21. He had flown more than 3,600 miles (5,790 kilometers) without stopping. People cheered the young hero wherever he went.

Lindbergh worked to improve airplane flight until his death in 1974. Today, you can see the *Spirit of St. Louis* at the Smithsonian Institution in Washington, D.C.

lion

The lion is one of the largest and most feared members of the cat family. A full-grown male lion may weigh 180 kilograms (400 pounds). He is easy to recognize because he has a mane of long hair on his head and shoulders. Females are smaller—about 135 kilograms (300 pounds)—and do not have manes. Neither do other members of the cat family.

Lions are carnivores—meat-eaters. For food, they kill antelope, zebras, and other mammals. They also eat animals that have died of disease or been killed by other hunters. Lions live on grassy plains. The lions' yellow-brown color blends well with the dry grasses. This makes it difficult for their prey—the animals they hunt—to see them.

Lions hunt mostly at night, but they may also hunt during the day. Usually, the females—lionesses—do the hunting. Sometimes they hunt alone, but usually several hunt together. They circle the prey and silently creep very close. Then one of the lions attacks. The prey runs, right toward the other lions. A lion can eat as much as 34 kilograms (75 pounds) of meat in a single meal. But a lion is fortunate to find such a large meal. It may not eat again for a week.

Lions do not hunt for fun. They kill only what they must eat.

Lions live in groups called *prides.* A pride consists of adults and their young. It may contain up to 35 animals. Members of a pride often "talk" to one another with purrs, moans, and mighty roars.

Baby lions are called *cubs.* At birth, they are blind and helpless. They are about the size of house cats. A mother lion takes good care of her cubs. When the cubs are able to walk, their mother begins to teach them how to hunt. When they are about a year old, they begin to join the older lions in chasing and killing prey.

Almost all lions live in Africa, south of the Sahara Desert. A few live in western India. Hundreds of years ago, lions also lived in southern Europe and the Middle East. Gradually, people drove the lions away. Today, many lions live in national parks, where hunting is not allowed.

Unlike many other wild animals, lions are easy to keep in zoos. They can be taught to do tricks and are popular circus animals. People admire the beauty and strength of these large cats. They agree with the people of 2,000 years ago who called the lion "the king of beasts."

See also **cat family.**

A female lion and her cubs are hunting for prey in the African grasslands. A male lion (top corner) has a shaggy mane.

liquid

When you pour orange juice from a pitcher, you are pouring a liquid. Liquid is a phase of matter between the solid phase and the gas phase.

The most familiar liquid on earth is water. Water is usually a liquid, but not always. If we cool it below 0° C (32° F), it turns into a solid—ice. If we heat it above 100° C (212° F), it turns into a gas—water vapor.

In some ways, liquids are like gases. Both liquids and gases take the shape of the containers they are in. Air in a room takes the shape of the room. Juice in a glass takes the shape of the glass.

But unlike a gas, a liquid cannot be pressed into a smaller space. If you close an empty plastic bottle tightly and squeeze it with your hands, the bottle will "give." The air can be pressed into a smaller space. But a closed plastic bottle completely full of water does not "give."

Unlike a gas, which cannot be poured and spreads upward and outward, a liquid can be poured and runs downhill. Rain that falls on high land runs downhill into streams. The streams run down to rivers. The rivers finally end at the sea. We use the force of this water running downhill to do work for us. Once, water power turned mill wheels, which turned millstones to grind flour. Today, we use its force to generate electricity.

Many solids can be turned into a liquid. If you heat some metals, they will melt and become liquid. Lead melts at 327.5° C (621.5° F). Iron melts at a much higher temperature—1,535° C (2,795° F). The temperature at which a solid turns into a liquid is called its *melting point.*

To turn a gas into a liquid, you need to take heat away from it—make it very cold. If you cool air below -190° C (-374° F), it will turn into liquid air. Scientists use liquid air and liquid oxygen in experiments.

If liquid air gets warmer than -190° C, it begins to bubble and turn into a gas. We call this the *boiling point* of air. All liquids have

PROPERTIES OF A LIQUID

A liquid takes the shape of its container.

A liquid cannot be squeezed into a smaller space.

A liquid can be poured.

A solid may become a liquid when heated.

A liquid may become a gas when heated.

a boiling point. Air has a very low boiling point. The boiling point of water is 100° C (212° F). The boiling point of lead is 1,740° C (3,164° F).

See also **gas; matter; solid;** and **water.**

Literature may be about heroes and heroines. King Arthur (left) is a hero of English stories and poems. Don Quixote (right) is a humorous hero in Spanish literature.

literature

Poems, plays, stories, and other written works that people read over and over again are called literature. Literature can make us think or make us laugh or cry. Literature can entertain us and teach us at the same time. Literature never gets old. Some great poems and plays were written more than 2,500 years ago yet seem fresh and new.

There are three main kinds of literature: poetry, fiction, and nonfiction.

Poetry Poetry is usually not written the way people normally speak. Poems often have special rhythms. Words at the ends of lines may rhyme with each other. Poets use language in new ways. They say things in ways that people remember.

Poems that tell a story are called **narrative poems.** They can be as long as a book. A few long narrative poems have been remembered for hundreds of years. Nearly 3,000 years ago, a poet named Homer composed a very long poem called the *Iliad.* It tells the story of a war between Greece and the city of Troy. Homer used the ancient Greek language, but the *Iliad* has been translated into many other languages, including English. Some people learn to read ancient Greek so that they can read Homer's great poem in his own words. (*See* **Homer.**)

Another long narrative poem, called *Beowulf,* was written in England around the year 600. We do not even know the poet's name, but he wrote in an early form of the English language called Old English. Old English is so different from the English we speak today that it is like a foreign language. *Beowulf* is about a knight who must kill a terrible monster named Grendel.

Short poems that describe the thoughts and feelings of the poet are called **lyric poems.** Lyric poems are sometimes like songs without music. Musicians sometimes set lyric poems to music. In fact, the words of a song are known as the *lyrics.*

Literature may be about the battle of good against evil. In the Narnia stories, four children (right) see this struggle in a magical kingdom (above).

Many beautiful lyric poems were written around 1800 by poets in England. William Wordsworth and John Keats are two of the most famous. Later in the 1800s, an American named Walt Whitman wrote a new kind of lyric poetry. About the same time, Emily Dickinson wrote many very short lyric poems. But for a long time she hid them away. People did not know that she was a poet for many years.

A very short kind of poetry that was first written in Japan is called *haiku*. A haiku always has 3 lines and 17 syllables. Many haiku have to do with nature and the seasons. (*See* **poetry**.)

Fiction Works of fiction are stories that writers make up, usually from their own imaginations. Even if part of a story is about real people, the storyteller imagines what they do and what they are thinking.

Written in March
by William Wordsworth

The cock is crowing
The stream is flowing,
The small birds twitter,
The lake doth glitter,
The green field sleeps in the sun;
The oldest and the youngest
Are at work with the strongest;
The cattle are grazing,
Their heads never raising;
There are forty feeding like one!

Like an army defeated
The snow hath retreated,
And now doth fare ill
On the top of the bare hill;
The ploughboy is whooping — anon —
There's joy in the mountains;
There's life in the fountains;
Small clouds are sailing,
Blue sky prevailing;
The rain is over and gone!

Almost every work of fiction has four basic things: characters, plot, theme, and style. The characters are the people in the story. The plot is what happens in the story. The theme is the main idea the writer had—perhaps the reason he or she thought up the story. The style is the way the writer tells the story. There are many kinds of fiction. The three main kinds of fiction are drama, novels, and short stories.

A **drama** is a story that is meant to be performed as a play by actors. The two main forms of drama are *tragedy* and *comedy*. A tragedy is a play that tells a sad story. A comedy is a play that tells a funny story, or at least a happy ending. (*See* **play.**)

The ancient Greeks wrote dramas about 2,500 years ago. We have copies of only about 30 of them. The Greeks performed these plays outdoors. They used music and dance as well as words. But we know only about the words.

Literature can be changed into many forms. *Oliver Twist*, a novel about a poor boy, was made into a musical called *Oliver!*

One of the greatest Greek plays is *Oedipus the King* by the writer Sophocles. Oedipus is told by an oracle—a person who speaks for the gods—that he will someday kill his father and marry his mother. Oedipus insists he will never do such a terrible thing. Many years later, he travels to a distant kingdom. There he kills the king and marries the queen. Then he discovers that he is their son. He has done what the oracle said he would do.

About 2,000 years after Sophocles, William Shakespeare was born in England. He became the greatest writer in the English language. His plays are performed wherever English is spoken. They have also been translated into many other languages. Shakespeare wrote both tragedies and comedies. Many were about kings and other famous people who lived long before Shakespeare's time. He followed old stories about what they did, but he had to imagine what they said and how they felt. (*See* **Shakespeare, William.**)

Another great writer of plays was writing in France at about the same time. His name was Jean Molière. Molière enjoyed making fun of people who were proud or greedy or had other faults.

A **novel** is a long story, usually with many characters and a complicated plot. It is not written in verse, and it is not meant to be performed by actors. But many novels have been made into movies later. *Mary Poppins,* by P. L. Travers, is just one example.

People have been reading novels since the 1700s. One early novel, Daniel Defoe's *Robinson Crusoe,* is about a man shipwrecked on an island for 24 years. It is one of the most popular books ever written in English.

Since Defoe's time, thousands of novels have been written in English, and thousands more in other languages. In the 1800s, great novels were written in Russia, France, England, and the United States.

There are several different kinds of novels. *Gothic* novels are stories of mystery and horror. A very famous early Gothic novel was

Frankenstein, which was written in 1818 by Mary Shelley. Many later novels and stories have used this idea about a creature created by a "mad scientist."

Science fiction novels are about imaginary events that happen in the future or on other planets or worlds.

Mystery novels are favorites of some readers. In a mystery novel, a crime has been committed, and a character in the story must find out who did it. Sherlock Holmes, the first famous detective, was the hero of mysteries written by Sir Arthur Conan Doyle. (*See* **Holmes, Sherlock.**)

Short stories are simpler than novels. Some are only a few pages long. Sometimes they are like fables—they have morals, or lessons. Sometimes they are like fairy tales.

Fairy tales are stories that were told by people for hundreds of years, even before there was writing. Parents told the stories to their children. The children told the stories to their children, and so on. Often a fairy tale tells about a prince or a princess who is growing up. It may have trolls, dwarfs, witches, and magic. The Grimm brothers collected many fairy tales in Germany in the 1800s. (*See* **fable; fairy tale;** and **Grimm brothers.**)

One early mystery story is *The Murders in the Rue Morgue* by the American writer Edgar Allan Poe. Sir Arthur Conan Doyle's Holmes was the main character in many short stories as well as in novels.

The American writer O. Henry amused his readers with surprise endings. For example, in one story, some people kidnap a rich little boy. They want to hold him for ransom. But the rich boy behaves so badly that the kidnappers pay ransom to the boy's parents to get rid of him.

Some other short stories tell how people live and think today. In fact, many science fiction stories are really about how today's world is shaping the future.

Nonfiction Nonfiction is about real events and people, not imaginary ones. One kind of nonfiction is **biography**—the story of a person's life. Most biographies are about famous men or women. When a person writes the story of his or her own life, the book is called an **autobiography.** A *diary* is a kind of autobiography telling events as they happen, day by day. One famous diary is *The Diary of Anne Frank,* written by a young girl who was in hiding with her family during World War II.

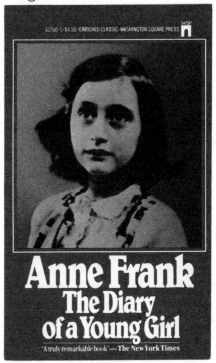

Anne Frank was a real girl. She kept a diary about hiding with her family from the Nazis during World War II.

Other nonfiction writing includes essays and speeches. An **essay** is usually a short piece that gives the writer's thoughts or opinions about some subject. Essays are like conversation. A good essay is entertaining and interesting even if you disagree with the writer.

Most speeches are remembered for only a few days or weeks after they are given. But sometimes a speech becomes a part of our literature. Many schoolchildren have memorized Abraham Lincoln's *Gettysburg Address.* It was a very short but beautiful speech he gave at that famous battlefield. (*See* **Lincoln, Abraham.**)

Another great speech was given by Martin Luther King, Jr. In Washington, D.C., in 1964, he told of his hopes for black people in the United States. "I have a dream. . ." he said. (*See* **King, Martin Luther, Jr.**)

Literature is an important subject in high schools and colleges. Reading and studying literature can be a good way to learn how to write better. It also helps the reader think about important subjects. Most of all, literature can take us on a trip to other places, past and future—even when we are sitting at home.

See also **American writers; English writers;** and **children's books.**

Lithuania, *see* Soviet Union

Little League baseball

Baseball has been popular ever since it was first played, over 100 years ago. In the United States, professional ballplayers play for teams of the National and American leagues. Since 1939, millions of children have played for leagues of their own—the Little Leagues.

The first Little League teams were formed in Williamsport, Pennsylvania. Today, more than 60,000 teams compete in 10,000 leagues in the United States and other countries. Little League players—both boys and girls—are between 8 and 12 years old. There are separate divisions for players aged 13 to 18 years old.

Most Little League rules are just like those of the major leagues. But youngsters play on a smaller diamond and use shorter bats. Also, games are 6 innings instead of 9.

Local leagues have 4 to 10 teams, each having 12 to 15 players. At the end of the regular season, all-star teams are chosen from league teams. The all-star teams compete in tournaments. Winners play in the Little League World Series, held each year in Williamsport.

See also **baseball.**

liver

The liver is the largest organ in the human body. In an adult, it weighs about 1.5 kilograms (3⅓ pounds). It is just above the stomach on the right side of the body. The liver helps with digestion and with keeping the blood clean.

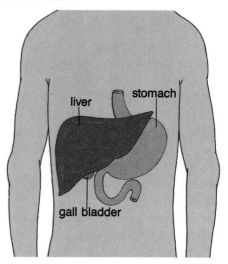

The liver is in the upper right part of the abdomen, across from the stomach.

The liver makes a brownish-green substance called *bile*. Bile is needed for the digestion of fatty foods. Bile passes out of the liver and into the gallbladder. When fatty foods are eaten, bile leaves the gallbladder and enters the small intestine to digest them. (*See* **digestion.**)

The liver cleans waste products and poisons from the blood. When drugs, medicines, or alcohol enter the body, they go to the liver. The liver changes them to harmless substances. But there is a limit to how many poisons the liver can remove from the body. If too much poison enters the body, the liver can be damaged. Then it will not work well. (*See* **blood circulation.**)

The liver also acts as a storehouse. It takes extra sugar out of the blood and changes it so it can be stored. When the body needs sugar, the liver releases what it has stored. The liver also stores iron and some vitamins, such as A, D, E, and K.

living things

Living things are all around you. You are a living thing. Your pets are living things. The plants, birds, insects, and worms in your yard are living things.

What is a Living Thing? All living things are alike in certain ways. They are made of cells. They use energy, and they grow. They reproduce to make more living things like themselves.

Some living things—such as bacteria, amebas, paramecia, and other protists—have only one cell. But most living things are made up of many cells. (*See* **cell; bacteria;** and **protist.**)

You know it takes energy to play and work. It also takes energy for you to stay alive and grow. All living things—animals, plants, fungi—use energy every minute.

All living things can reproduce. The offspring grow up to look very much like the parents. (*See* **reproduction.**)

When you were born, you were probably about 46 centimeters (18 inches) long and weighed about 2.75 kilograms (6 pounds). Today, you are much larger and still growing. All living things grow as a result of the activities of their cells. Some nonliving things, such as crystals, grow, too. But they do not grow because of the activities of cells. (*See* **growth, human.**)

Groups of Living Things There are millions of kinds of living things. Early humans may have put living things into three groups. Those that could be eaten may have made one group. Those that could not or should not be eaten may have been put in another group. Those that might eat humans could have made up the third group.

Later, people divided living things into groups according to different rules. For example, living things that moved were called "animals." Those that did not move were called "plants." This kind of division was used for a long time.

As scientists studied living things more, they saw that this way of grouping—classifying—things was not good, either. Certain living things, such as corals and barnacles, do not move. But, like animals, they must get their energy by eating food. Scientists moved corals and barnacles from the plant group to the animal group. For centuries, fungi were classified as plants. Like plants, they do not move, and their cells are similar to the cells of plants. But fungi cannot make their own food, as plants do. Today, we do not group fungi with plants. (*See* **coral** and **fungus.**)

	can move by itself	can feed and grow	can reproduce
LIVING THINGS	YES	YES	YES
NONLIVING THINGS	NO	NO	NO

FIVE KINGDOMS OF LIVING THINGS

Monerans

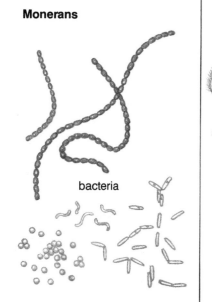

bacteria

Protists

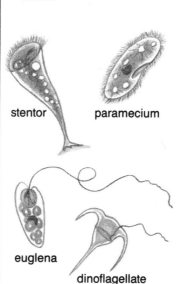

stentor   paramecium

euglena

dinoflagellate

Fungi

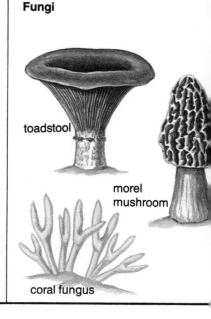

toadstool

morel mushroom

coral fungus

Five Kingdoms Today, scientists divide living things into five groups, called *kingdoms.* These kingdoms are based on how living things get their food and on the kinds of cells they have.

The simplest living things are those in the *moneran* kingdom. This kingdom includes all of the bacteria. A moneran has only a single cell. This cell is very simple, and it is

These tiny single-celled creatures called diatoms are part of the moneran kingdom.

different from the cells of all other living things. Some monerans make their food and others get food from their surroundings. (*See* **moneran.**)

Protists make another kingdom. A protist, too, is made up of only one cell. But the cell of a protist is more complex than the cell of a moneran. Many protists chase and catch food in their watery environment. Other protists can make their own food. Billions of these protists live in ocean water near the surface. They are important in ocean food chains. (*See* **protist** and **food chain.**)

Fungi are so different from plants that they are now in their own kingdom. They have complex cells with cell walls. They take their food from the environment.

Plants form another kingdom. Plants have many complex cells. Each plant cell has a wall around it. Most plants have green leaves and stems where they make food. (*See* **plant.**)

Animals are the fifth kingdom of living things. Their bodies are made of many complex cells without cell walls. All animals have to get food from their environment. (*See* **animal.**)

Some living things do not fit well into any kingdom. Slime molds are one example.

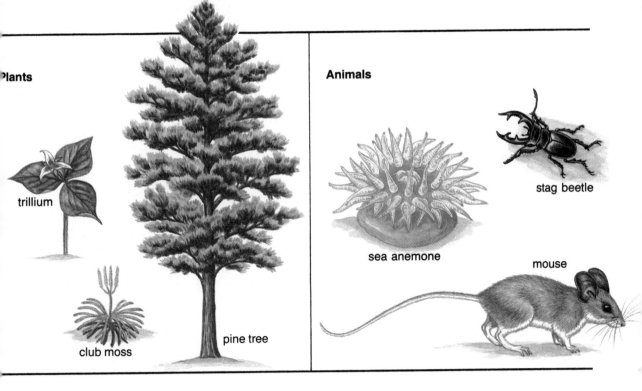

Plants

trillium

club moss

pine tree

Animals

sea anemone

stag beetle

mouse

During part of their life cycle, slime molds are like fungi. During another part, they are like protists. Today, they are grouped with fungi. Someday, scientists may make a new kingdom just for the slime molds.

lizard

Lizards are reptiles. They are related to snakes, turtles, and alligators. Most lizards are less than 37 centimeters (15 inches) long. The largest lizard is the Komodo dragon, a monitor lizard that lives in Indonesia. It may be as long as 3 meters (10 feet) and weigh as much as 135 kilograms (300 pounds).

Lizards live in all parts of the world except the polar regions. There are about 3,000 kinds. Most live on the ground. Some spend most of their time in trees. They may have special pads on their feet to help them stick to smooth surfaces.

Lizards have long tails. A lizard uses its tail for balance or to hold on to twigs when climbing. Most lizards can break off their tails. If the lizard is attacked, it leaves its tail wiggling on the ground. This holds the attention of the enemy while the lizard runs away. The lizard soon grows a new tail.

Chameleons and some other kinds of lizards can change color. This helps them blend into the background, so enemies and prey—the animals they hunt—cannot see them.

Lizards are very important to people, especially to farmers, because they eat large numbers of insects.

See also **chameleon** and **reptile**.

This collared lizard has collarlike black and red markings around its neck.

lobster

Lobsters belong to a group of animals called *crustaceans.* The lobster has a hard outer shell made of many pieces joined together by thin, soft sections. (*See* **crustacean.**)

Lobsters are the largest crustaceans. Some weigh more than 11 kilograms (25 pounds). True lobsters have two large pinching claws on their front legs. These lobsters live off the eastern coast of North America. Another kind lives off the western coast. It is called a *spiny lobster* because its shell is covered with spines. It does not have large pincers.

Lobsters spend their days in burrows hidden among rocks or other things on the ocean floor. They come out at night to feed. They eat both plants and animals. When they outgrow their shells, lobsters must *molt* —shed their shells. Underneath the old shell, a new one has been forming.

A lot of people enjoy eating lobsters, so lobster fishing is an important industry.

This lobster is almost invisible as it crawls along the ocean floor.

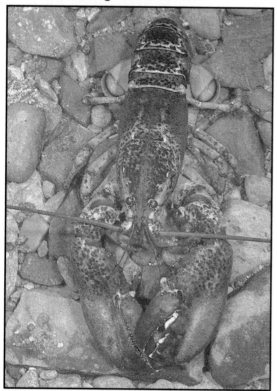

London Bridge stretches across the Thames River. An earlier London Bridge was taken apart and rebuilt at Lake Havasu, Arizona.

London

London is the capital city of the United Kingdom. It is in southeastern England, along the banks of the Thames (TEMZ) River. Nearly 7 million people live in the 32 boroughs—self-governing districts—of London. That makes it the largest city in Europe.

London is a world center of business and banking. As capital of the United Kingdom, it is also an important center of government. The people of England, Scotland, Wales, and Northern Ireland elect representatives to Parliament, which meets in London. The leader of the government—the prime minister—is a member of Parliament.

London's history dates back many centuries. Nearly 2,000 years ago, Roman armies invaded Britain. One of the towns they set up was called Londinium. Remains of a wall that surrounded the old city 1,000 years ago still stand in London today.

One of London's oldest buildings is the Tower of London. It was built between the

"Wimbledon," the name of the London suburb where it is played—is the oldest and most famous tennis championship tournament in the world. Other favorite British sports include soccer (which Londoners call football) and rugby, a game something like American football.

London, Jack

Jack London was an American writer of adventure stories. He was born in San Francisco, California, in 1876. He had to quit school when he was 14 to help support his family. When he was 19, he entered high school. He worked hard, and in a year he was accepted in college. But after only one term, he went to work as a seaman and sailed to Japan. Years later, Jack wrote about his adventures in *The Sea-Wolf.*

After coming back to California, London rushed to Canada in 1897 to try to make his fortune during the Klondike gold rush. He did not find gold, but he wrote stories about life in the Far North. They were collected in a book called *The Son of the Wolf.* It was a great success.

London's most famous book, *The Call of the Wild,* is about the Far North, too. The

years 1000 and 1100 and was used as a prison. Today, the beautiful jewels of the British royal family are on display there.

In 1666, most of the city was destroyed by a fire. It was soon rebuilt, but many of its buildings were destroyed again during World War II. Between 1940 and 1945, the city was bombed night after night by German planes. (*See* **World War II.**)

Ceremony and tradition are important parts of London life. For example, hundreds of people gather every morning to watch the traditional "changing of the guard" in front of Buckingham Palace, where the royal family lives. The guards are dressed in bright red uniforms. One team of guards replaces another in a military ceremony.

London is also famous for its theaters, concert halls, and museums. In the late 1500s, William Shakespeare wrote his plays for a theater in London. Since then, many other great writers have lived in London. The city has long been a favorite place for musicians. Some of the world's greatest art is displayed in London museums.

Many Londoners are sports fans. The British Open Tennis Tournament—known as

Jack London led an exciting life. Many of his stories were based on his adventures.

hero of the story is a dog, Buck. Buck is stolen from his California family and taken to the Klondike. He survives as a sled dog despite his harsh surroundings. After his master is killed, Buck turns wild and becomes the leader of a wolf pack.

Jack London succeeded at making a good living by his writing. But he was always restless and looking for change. He died when he was only 40, in 1916.

longitude, *see* latitude and longitude

Los Angeles

Los Angeles is a large city on the coast of southern California. To its west and south are the beautiful beaches of the Pacific Ocean. To its northeast are the snowcapped San Gabriel Mountains. The area has very little rainfall, but it is very green. *Aqueducts*—big water pipes—bring water to Los Angeles all the way from the Colorado River and from northern California.

Los Angeles itself covers 465 square miles (1,204 square kilometers) and has more than 3 million people. But more than 100 smaller towns and cities surround Los Angeles. All together, this huge cluster of cities has more than 12 million people. It is the second-largest urban region in the United States. Only the New York City region has more people.

Los Angeles was founded in 1781 by 44 settlers from the Spanish colony of Mexico. They named the town El Pueblo de Nuestra Señora la Reina de Los Angeles. This means "The Town of Our Lady the Queen of the Angels," a name for Mary, the mother of Jesus. Later, people shortened the name to simply Los Angeles—"The Angels."

The colony of farmers and ranchers grew slowly at first. In 1850, nearly 70 years after it was founded, little Los Angeles had only 1,610 people. In that year, California became a state in the United States.

Hollywood, the movie capital of the world, is really a neighborhood in Los Angeles.

In 1885, a railroad running from Chicago to Los Angeles was completed. To get customers, the railroad dropped the fare as low as $1. Soon, trainloads of settlers were coming from the Midwest. In the late 1800s, oil wells were dug all over Los Angeles. The city built a harbor so the oil could be shipped easily. A skinny strip of land connects the harbor to Los Angeles. By 1900, Los Angeles was a small city.

The city grew and spread quickly in the 1920s. People came for the warm, gentle climate and to make money. Many new neighborhoods were built, and connected by railroads. Los Angeles became the home of a new business—movies. California's good weather made it easy to shoot movies most of the year. The movie industry centered around Hollywood, one of the small towns in the area. By the 1930s, Hollywood was one of the most glamorous towns in the world.

The region around Los Angeles grew fastest between 1950 and 1965. During these years, more than 1,000 new settlers arrived every day. Thousands of new businesses were started and hundreds of new schools were built. Los Angeles, its surrounding towns, and the state of California planned a system of highways to replace the old railroads. These highways, called *freeways,* are famous for their graceful design. People in

Los Angeles drive from place to place on these giant, busy freeways.

Los Angeles and Chicago, Illinois are the two largest manufacturing centers in the nation. Los Angeles is the largest producer of aircraft, spacecraft, and other aerospace equipment.

Los Angeles attracts millions of visitors each year. They come to see Hollywood and its movie studios, and to spend time at the beaches. They visit the mountains, and such world-famous attractions as Disneyland, in the nearby city of Anaheim.

Unfortunately, Los Angeles is also known for its air pollution. Even the Indians called the Los Angeles area "Valley of the Smoke." The mountains trapped warm, smoky air in the valley. Later, the waste gases from millions of cars were trapped there, too. This helped to form *smog*—a kind of air pollution. Los Angeles has passed laws to reduce smog. No one may burn trash in the region, and all cars must have smog-control devices. Similar laws were later passed in other parts of the United States. (*See* **air pollution.**)

Louis XIV

Louis was a popular name for the kings of France. The Louis who became king in 1643 was the 14th monarch with that name. This Louis—Louis XIV—was only four years old when he became king. His mother ruled for him while he was young. When Louis grew up, he became so powerful and his court was so splendid that he was called the "Sun King."

Louis XIV is most famous for the palace he had built at Versailles, a town about 10 miles (16 kilometers) from Paris. This palace has more than 1,000 rooms, and beautiful gardens that seem to go on for miles. Louis burned the records so no one could ever find out how much the palace cost. The palace was grand, but life there was not always comfortable. In winter, the palace was so cold that water sometimes froze in the glasses during dinner parties.

Louis XIV was king for more than 70 years. During his long reign, France was the strongest nation in the world. The French language became the language of diplomacy in Europe. Louis had a large army, and it fought in several wars. The wars did not gain much for France, and they cost many lives and millions of dollars. Still, the people of France consider Louis XIV one of their greatest leaders.

Louis XIV (right) built the elegant palace at Versailles. Rooms like the one below were decorated by great artists chosen by the king.

Louisiana

Capital: Baton Rouge
Area: 47,752 square miles (123,676 square kilometers) (31st-largest state)
Population (1980): 4,206,098 (1985): about 4,481,000 (18th-largest state)
Became a state: April 30, 1812 (18th state)

Louisiana is a state in the southeastern United States. It is shaped like a high-top sneaker. The bottom of the sneaker is on the Gulf of Mexico.

Land Louisiana is one of the flattest states in the nation. The Mississippi River winds through Louisiana and empties into the Gulf of Mexico. The soil is very fertile along the Mississippi and other rivers in Louisiana. In the south, there are many swampy "bayous," which are actually slow-moving streams. (*See* **Mississippi River.**)

Louisiana's climate is hot and humid. Southeastern Louisiana receives up to 60 inches (150 centimeters) of rain each year.

The Gulf coast along Louisiana has many large bays. The bays are lined with marshes. In some places, "land islands" rise out of the marshes. They are about 100 feet (30.5 meters) high and 1 mile (1.6 kilometers) across. Great deposits of salt or petroleum lie under their domes.

Louisiana ranks second in the nation in oil and gas production. Petroleum comes from wells throughout the state and out in the Gulf of Mexico as well as from the marsh areas. The petroleum is sent to a refinery near Baton Rouge. It is the largest oil refinery in the world.

Only one state—Florida—produces more sugarcane than does Louisiana. Cotton, soybeans, and rice are other crops. Louisiana also leads the nation in the production of

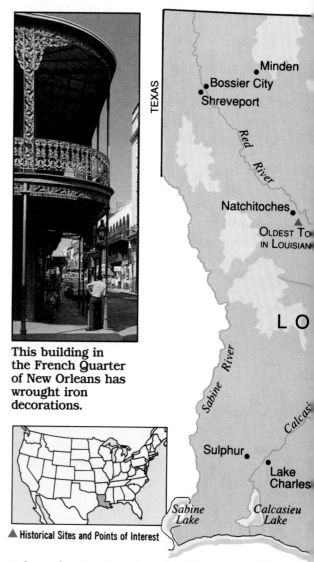

This building in the French Quarter of New Orleans has wrought iron decorations.

▲ Historical Sites and Points of Interest

oak and other hardwoods. Fur, especially muskrat, is another major product.

History Spanish explorers discovered Louisiana in the early 1500s, but did not claim the territory for Spain. Late in the 1600s, the French explorer La Salle recognized the value of the Mississippi River for transportation. He claimed the land for France and named it after King Louis XIV. French settlers came, and then Spanish settlers. Their descendants are called *Creoles.* (*See* **La Salle, Sieur de.**)

Starting in 1719, slaves were brought from Africa to work the cotton and sugarcane plantations. In the second half of the 1700s, about 5,000 French people from eastern Canada arrived. They settled along the bayous of southern Louisiana. Their descendants are called *Cajuns.*

It took Louisiana a long time to recover from the Civil War. The construction of railroads and the clearing of shipping channels helped the state become important again in trade and transportation.

People Rural Louisiana Cajuns are noted for their language—a blend of French and English—their music, and their food. The spicy food of the city Creoles is famous, too.

Today, more than two-thirds of the people in the state of Louisiana live in cities. Baton Rouge is Louisiana's capital and second-largest city. About 538,000 people live in or around Baton Rouge. It is an important port on the Mississippi River. It is a large

Magnolia

Eastern brown pelican

Ownership of Louisiana passed back and forth between France and Spain until 1803. In that year, it was sold to the United States as part of the Louisiana Purchase. (*See* **Louisiana Purchase.**)

Louisiana was one of the first states to join the Confederate States of America just before the Civil War. Its people and economy suffered terribly during that war. Its major city and port, New Orleans, was captured in 1862 and occupied by the Union Army until the war was over. (*See* **Civil War.**)

petroleum and chemical center.

New Orleans is the largest city in Louisiana. About 1,318,800 people live in or near New Orleans. It is a major trade and industrial center. It is also the second-busiest port in the nation.

New Orleans is famous for its French Quarter, its jazz music, and its Mardi Gras celebration. Each year, just before the holy season of Lent, people come from all over the world to join in the Mardi Gras parades and fabulous costume balls.

Louisiana Purchase

The Louisiana Purchase of 1803 was probably the greatest land bargain in history. Through it, the United States bought a vast piece of land extending from the Mississippi River to the Rocky Mountains. The Louisiana Purchase doubled the size of the young nation.

Spain had recently given the land, called the Louisiana Territory, to France. Napoleon, the ruler of France, dreamed of creating a powerful French colonial empire in Louisiana. He already had plans to take control of New Orleans, a busy port at the mouth of the Mississippi River.

The Mississippi River was the western boundary of the United States and an important trade route. Western farmers and fur trappers shipped their goods down the Mississippi and through New Orleans. Traders bringing goods up the Mississippi passed through New Orleans, too. It was very important that Americans be able to use New Orleans as a port.

President Thomas Jefferson worried that Napoleon might close New Orleans to American trade. So he told Robert R. Livingston, the U.S. minister to France, to try to buy New Orleans. But Napoleon would not hear of it.

Fortunately for the United States, events helped change Napoleon's mind. The French ruler knew that he would soon go to war with Britain. Such a war would cost a great deal of money. He also learned that the Americans might try to take New Orleans by force. He realized he might lose it and get nothing in return.

Jefferson sent James Monroe to help Livingston buy New Orleans. Jefferson said they could offer Napoleon up to $10 million for New Orleans and some nearby land.

By now, Napoleon's need for money was greater than his desire for a colonial empire. He surprised the American ministers by offering to sell not only New Orleans but also the Louisiana Territory for $15 million. Monroe and Livingston quickly accepted, even though the price was greater than what they

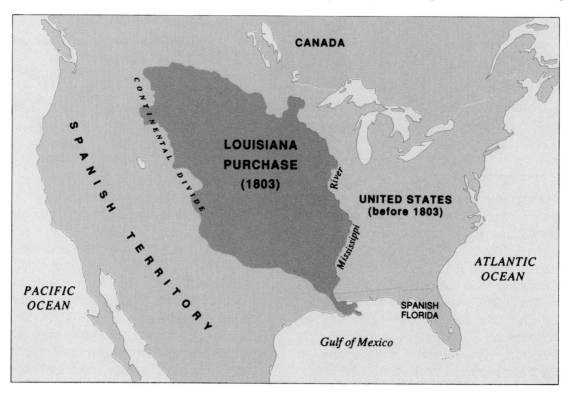

were supposed to spend. On May 2, 1803, they signed the treaty that made the Louisiana Territory part of the United States. Later, Congress approved the treaty.

The Louisiana Purchase added about 828,000 square miles (2,144,520 square kilometers) of land to the United States. In time, this region would form all or part of 15 states.

See also **Napoleon**; **Jefferson, Thomas**; and **Lewis and Clark Expedition**.

lumber, *see* wood

lung

All the cells of your body need oxygen to burn food. When your cells burn food for energy, they produce carbon dioxide and water. Your body must get rid of these waste products. Your lungs are specially built to supply the oxygen that your body cells need. The lungs also get rid of carbon dioxide and some of the water that your body cells produce. (*See* **blood circulation**.)

You have two lungs, one on each side of your chest, inside your rib cage. The lungs are cone-shaped organs, each about the size of a football. In children, the lungs are a pinkish color. In adults, however, they turn grayish white from dust and dirt that has built up over the years. The lungs feel spongy and very light because they contain millions of tiny air sacs.

When you breathe, air travels down the *trachea,* a tube sometimes called the windpipe. The trachea divides in two to form the *bronchial tubes.* Each bronchial tube leads to a lung. In the lungs, the tubes divide again and again, until they are very small.

At the end of the smallest tubes are tiny, air-filled sacs. These sacs are much too small to be seen with the naked eye. When they are magnified, they look like tiny clusters of grapes. The wall of each air sac is only one cell thick. These moist air sacs are surrounded by tiny blood vessels. Gases can

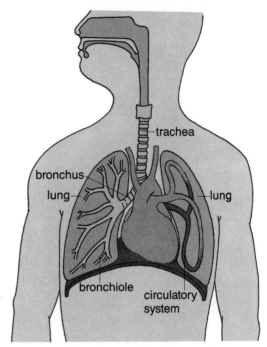

The lungs fill most of the chest cavity, and are protected by the ribs.

easily pass through the walls of the air sacs and the blood vessels.

When you breathe in, your chest expands. Fresh air fills the air sacs, and they blow up like tiny balloons. Some of the oxygen in the fresh air passes from the air sacs into the bloodstream. At the same time, carbon dioxide and water from the bloodstream pass into the air sacs. When you breathe out, air high in carbon dioxide and water leaves the lungs. (*See* **breathing**.)

Diseases of the lungs make breathing difficult, so the body gets less oxygen. Pneumonia is caused by an infection of the lungs. Bronchitis is caused by an infection of the bronchial tubes. Asthma may be caused by an allergic reaction. Emphysema and lung cancer are two very serious lung diseases that can cause death. We do not know the exact causes of these diseases. But we know that smoking greatly increases the chances of developing emphysema or lung cancer. (*See* **cancer**.)

Luther, Martin

Martin Luther was a leader of the Protestant Reformation. He and other people in Europe protested—argued against—the teachings

95

Martin Luther was a religious leader who helped begin the Protestant Reformation.

and practices of the Roman Catholic Church. They broke away from the Catholic Church and started their own churches. (*See* **Protestant churches.**)

Luther was born in 1483, in the German city of Eisleben. His father, a miner, wanted his son to have a good education. Luther went to school and later became a priest and university professor.

In Europe during the early 1500s, the Roman Catholic Church was very strong. Many people, including princes, followed its teachings and obeyed its rules. But Luther disagreed with some of the Church's beliefs and practices. One day in 1517, he nailed a paper to the door of the Catholic church in Wittenberg, a German town. This paper—called the "Ninety-five Theses"—listed 95 practices that Luther disagreed with.

Luther translated the Bible into German. His translation is so beautiful that it helped to form the modern German language and is still read today. He also preached, and wrote long letters and songs.

Luther died in 1546. After his death, his followers started a church that became known as the Lutheran Church.

Luxembourg, *see* **Europe**

---

lynx

The lynx is a wild member of the cat family. It is much smaller than a lion, tiger, or leopard, and has a very short tail. But it has long legs and large feet. Males are bigger than females. A male lynx may be a meter (39 inches) long and weigh more than 20 kilograms (45 pounds).

A lynx has a black-striped ruff—a furry collar—on the sides of its face. Its large, pointed ears have long black hairs on their tips. The fur of a lynx is thick and very soft. People kill lynx for their fur.

Lynx live in dense forests in Canada and the northern United States. They also live in northern Europe and Asia. The thick fur keeps the animals warm during the cold winters. The broad feet are like snowshoes. They help the lynx walk on top of the snow.

Lynx are carnivores—meat-eaters—and hunt mostly at night. Their main foods are rabbits and hares. They also hunt mice, squirrels, and birds.

Lynx live alone for most of the year. In early spring, males and females find one another and mate. About two months later, the females give birth to one to five kittens. Lynx kittens are as playful as house kittens. The mothers take good care of their young and teach them how to hunt.

See also **cat family.**

The lynx, like other cats, is a hunter. Here it stalks a rabbit.